Forward

This book is meant to be a resource, guide, motivation and inspiration to those who desire to reach their preparedness goals. Primarily this book focuses on food storage & preparedness and teaches how to buy, make, store, and use your food storage. However, there are other aspects of preparedness that this book touches on.

Our motto "It is better to be prepared and prevent than to repair and repent" is our main focus because in any situation it is better to have something and not need it than to need it and not have it. The security that comes with being prepared- especially if something is needed is priceless.

What are you waiting for?
Join us!

Dedication

This book is dedicated to my mom, who is probably the world's most talented person and taught me the value of being prepared. She taught many classes on preparedness and had thought about writing a book, but with 9 kids she didn't have the time. Her desire to write a book like this motivated me to fulfill that dream and I am grateful for all the skills, experience and knowledge she shared with me. Her encouragement motivated me to write this book and accomplish my goals.

About the Author

JoDee Martin is the youngest of 9 children and a mom of 6 children. She was raised in a small rural town in Utah where preparedness and food storage were high priority in her family. Since the nearest store was 30 miles away, she learned that it's better to have something and not need it then to need something and not have it. Education is also something she is passionate about, so she has spent a lot of her life learning new things and obtaining many different certifications and experiences including: Rapid Eye Technology, EMT basic and intermediate, state trainer for victim advocates, high school sign language teacher, public speaking, graphic & webpage design, social media management, business consulting, marketing, book author, and anything else she has the opportunity to learn or do.

She has written a number of books mostly being the children's books that started her writing career writing them for her children when they were very young. From there she wrote this book, assembled a cook book, and a book for stay at home moms to find ways to make money from home.

Come join the Facebook group that aligns with this book and uses it's teachings split up into course units as well as a community of members to share information. The group can be found at:
www.facebook.com/groups/foodstorage101

JoDee is the owner of 2 blogs, "A to Z for Moms Like Me" covers a variety of topics of interest to women, and "What 8 Ate" which is all about feeding her family of 8 on a budget.
You can follow her blogs at these addresses:
www.atozformomslikeme.blogspot.com
www.what8ate.com
Facebook & Instagram @Atozformomslikeme and @What8ate
Pinterest @Atozformoms and @what8ate

JoDee is also a Thrive Life Food Consultant and loves giving customers the opportunity to purchase freeze dried foods at wholesale prices. Her website is: www.what8ate.thrivelife.com

Unlike most people, JoDee enjoys public speaking and loves sharing her knowledge with others. If you would like to have her speak at an event please email her at:
atozformomslikeme@gmail.com

Introduction

~By small and simple things are great things brought to pass~

We live our lives one day at a time, because taking things one week or month at a time isn't an option! So focus on that, one day at a time. Things in nature all happen little by little one day at a time. You don't plant an apple seed one day and expect it to be a full tree producing apples the same day or even the next day. But with the small and steady and constant growth of an apple seed, after **years** it becomes a full tree producing apples of its own. The seed will not grow into a tree though without consistent nurture of the things it needs in order to grow. Water, sun, and soil are as essential to a seed's growth as daily nurturing of spiritual and temporal things are to our growth and success.

"We can begin ever so modestly. We can begin with a one week's food supply and gradually build it to a month, and then to three months. ... I fear that so many feel that a long-term food supply is so far beyond their reach that they make no effort at all." Pres Hinckley[1]

---

[1] "To Men of the Priesthood," *Liahona* and *Ensign*, Nov. 2002, 58

With all things spiritual or temporal it is better to prepare and prevent, than to repair and repent. There are so many similar sayings: "better safe than sorry" "just in case" "It's better to be a day early with a dollar extra than a day late and a dollar short". No one ever dies saying "if only I wasn't so prepared!" preparedness is something that is never wasted, but lack of preparedness can mean extreme consequences. So they can all be summed up as: "It's better to have something and not need it, than to need it and not have it."

From President Thomas S. Monson, First Counselor, we hear: "Many more people could ride out the storm-tossed waves in their economic lives if they had their year's supply of food … and were debt-free. Today we find that many have followed this counsel in reverse: they have at least a year's supply of debt and are food-free."[1]

---

[1] "That Noble Gift—Love at Home," *Church News*, May 12, 2001, 7

Why Should I?

"Someone has said it was not raining when Noah built the ark. But he built it, and the rains came." The Lord has said, "If ye are prepared ye shall not fear." (D&C 38:30) Pres. Hinckley[1]

We have been told by our prophets for years to be prepared. We have more resources at our fingertips than any other nation or people in the history of the world. We have scriptures, we have the *Ensign*, church websites, the ability to watch conference and listen to the words of our prophet and apostles, we can literally search for the answer to any question on our phones we carry with us and find any recipe or idea on pinterest. Saying "we weren't told" or "we didn't know how" doesn't hold any water!

Our mentality has become one of entitlement, selfishness, and laziness. Those are not traits that are natural to our spirit. You are not entitled to have a place to live, food, water, clothes, and so on. Those are privileges that can be taken away if you do not earn them and provide them for yourself. If something were to happen and you chose not to heed the prophet's warnings to have food storage you and your family would suffer the consequences. You are one of hundreds of millions. Since

---

[1] "If ye are prepared ye shall not fear," *Ensign*, Oct. 2005

you're just another number to the government, they will not and cannot prioritize you and your family's needs at the top of their list. The church, although it has the best structure and organization for taking care of others, is not able to fully provide for all its members in time of need. It is up to you. If you are a parent, you are responsible for your children and your preparedness or lack thereof could mean the difference between life and death for them.

Ok, now that I've gone all dooms-day on you, let me assure you there is hope! Things don't have to happen overnight. Focus on one day at a time and what you can do that day to improve your preparedness - physically, spiritually, mentally and financially. If you do just one small thing in each of those areas you will be following the counsel of our Prophets and you will be amazed at the blessings that will be poured out on you and your family. Little by little, do your part. Show Heavenly Father by your daily actions that you desire to obey and he will bless you tremendously.

In this book I have added a weekly guide for an entire year that outlines simple easy tasks you can do each week to reach your ultimate goals. The guide includes the most common goals people have, however if your goals are not listed then simply take the same approach and break down your ultimate goal into weekly goals that are achievable and will keep the momentum towards the ultimate goal. We also have a facebook group called "52 weeks of Little by Little" that is free and offers support and encouragement from others like you who are working towards their goals. Come join the group!

"We continue to encourage members to store sufficient food, clothing, and where possible fuel for at least one year. We have not laid down an exact formula for what should be stored. However, we suggest that members concentrate on essential foods that sustain life, such as grains, legumes, cooking oil, powdered milk, salt, sugar or honey, and water. Most families can achieve and maintain this basic level of preparedness. The decision to do more than this rests with the individual." Home Storage: Build on the Basics", *Ensign*, June 1989, 39

Mental Preparedness

It's time for a change in attitude! Your attitude determines your altitude. Shifting your perception from one of entitlement to one of accountability, responsibility, and independence can be overwhelming. Our perception is based on our personal experiences and environment. Changing how we see those experiences can then change our perceptions.

There is a story I learned when becoming a Certified Rapid Eye Technician.

Once upon a time there was a farmer whose fence was knocked down and his prized horse escaped. His neighbor came over and said to him "that's too bad about your horse, if only the fence hadn't been knocked down" to which the farmer replied "how do I know it was a bad thing?" A few days later his prized horse returned with a dozen wild mustangs just as valuable. The neighbor then came over and exclaimed "what good fortune! Your prized horse brought back more with him!" to which the farmer replied "how do I know it's a good thing?" The next week the farmer's son decided to ride and train one of the horses and in the process was thrown off breaking his leg. The neighbor came over again saying "that's too bad about your son breaking his leg, if only the mustangs hadn't joined the return of your prized horse" to which the farmer replied "how do I know it's a bad thing?" Two weeks later the army marched through town enlisting every able bodied young man into the war, because the farmers son had a broken leg he was not forced to enlist. And so the story goes.

The moral of this story is that even though the perception of the neighbor changed with each set of circumstances, the farmer knew that things just happen and it was up to him to choose to see them as good or bad.

Mental preparedness includes pondering worst-case scenarios, planning what to do in the event of a disaster. Knowing where your family would go, what you would do, how you would survive, who you would be with, and so on. Understanding that all things happen for a reason and all you can do is be prepared to the best of your ability, and the rest is up to Heavenly Father.

Education is another key to mental preparedness. Educating yourself in what to do in case of an emergency could save you or someone you love's life. Learn survival skills, cooking skills, emergency medical skills, handy man skills, sewing skills, automotive skills and all other skills your family needs and uses. Learning how to fix things around the house, basic plumbing or electrical problem solving, building, and other household skills can be very valuable for both the present as well as in case of an emergency. Take every opportunity to learn something new that you can from others. Knowledge is power, and the combined knowledge of many will complete the skills and development needed for society in the future. Do not count on someone always being around to pay to fix, build, make, or do something for you. When it comes down to necessity you may not have money or items to trade for payment, or there may not be anyone with the desired knowledge to help.

My husband and I were talking one day about the last days and how many people inside and outside the church strongly advise to not have debt, but we were talking about how when there is some sort of huge collapse (whatever it may be) that money and debt most-likely wont be used or an issue. (this is our opinions so I don't have evidence to back it up, but just our thoughts)

So we talked about why it would be stressed by so many and so important to not have debt when at the end of the day when something drastic does happen it wont matter. Then we realized, it's not a matter of the debt existing or not, but a matter of the mentality that comes with having debt vs not. Debt equals a "buy now, pay later" mentality. Spending more than you have, keeping up with the Joneses, and literally reaping before you sew anything.

We concluded that it is the mentality that will prove detrimental when something drastic happens. Those who have a debt mentality and are used to getting the reward before the work will have a hard reality to face when the work HAS to come before the reward. When planting a garden and months of labor have to happen in order to feed their family, when a house has to be built with their own two hands, time and sacrifice before their family has a place to live. In the mean time while the work is being done, the sacrifices of going without are made. What a wake-up call to a generation that has become entitled and constantly given instant gratification! It is a mental preparedness reality I hadn't thought of before, and a little scary when I think of the world my kids are growing up in.

We are all guilty of having this mentality to some degree. Debt or not, most people are dependent on internet, cars, paychecks, electricity, grocery stores, etc. What would your family do if those were all gone?

Wouldn't it be better to be prepared for the "what if" than to suffer the "when"?

One of the ways we can prepare ourselves now and keep ourselves grounded when it comes to mental preparedness is by having occasional fasts from things such as spending, internet, phones, etc. It also helps us reflect on and sometimes reprioritize things in our life.

Spiritual Preparedness

"We encourage you to follow this counsel with the assurance that a people prepared through obedience to the commandments of God need not fear." (Letter to priesthood leaders, 24 June 1988.)

As important as temporal food storage is, spiritual preparedness is just as important. How many times have the scriptures talked about feeding our spirit? It is not a coincidence that using food references as an example of something our spirit needs was used. Just as our bodies need food to survive, our spirit need to be nourished or it will die (meaning become disconnected from Heavenly Father).

Spiritual nourishment comes from the things we do daily. Reading our scriptures, praying, going to church, and following the prophet's guidance-- these are all simple instructions, but just as drinking water and eating food every day is a simple task, these simple tasks of obedience are necessary for our spiritual survival. You wouldn't stop drinking water in order to stay alive because it was just too easy, yet the easy things to take care of our spirit get overlooked.

Unlike our physical bodies, getting spiritually "fat" isn't a bad or unhealthful thing! There's no such thing as being "too" close to the spirit, and being "too" righteous. In fact, our bodies are only with us until we die, where as our spirit is with us forever, so which should get more tender-loving-care? Would you take better care of an outfit you wear than you would your skin?

I was once told that when the scriptures repeat themselves it's because it's something VERY important and that we should pay attention. It is no small coincidence that there are so many comparisons to "seeds" in the scriptures. Faith is like a seed, parable of the seeds, faith of a mustard seed, and so on. Think about it-- why would Heavenly Father and Jesus Christ want us to understand things compared to a seed? Well, seeds grow slowly. They require a lot of care and attention. And then, over time with continuous care and attention to their needs they become something great, productive, and very desirable.

So many things are like a seed. Our spirits, bodies, how we learn, our relationships, our testimony, and so on. All starting so small and needing consistent care and attention. And when given the needed care and attention they all can become something great and desirable.   Time works like a seed, slowly, at its own pace. And time is infinite. We have an abundance of time, when managed properly, and yet still need to put in efforts constantly to grow and learn in the things that will take us in the direction we desire in life.

You can't rush growth and enlightenment, but you can guarantee them over time with consistent care and attention little by little. Line upon line, precept upon precept-- sound familiar? Just as we were born babies and grew a little each day to become the adult in the body we now have, little by little we gain spiritual enlightenment when we are following the commandments and doing the things to nourish our spirit little by little.

Spiritual procrastination is like planned death-bed conversion. At that point there is no more time on this earth to learn and grow and achieve more spiritual enlightenment. Oh what wasted time! Imagine if you planned to do the same to your physical body-- refuse to eat until just before your body is ready to die. To eat food at that point is pointless; it will not save your physical body from the damage done over time just by eating one meal at the end. Remember, little by little works for progression as well as regression. **You can little by little draw away from the Savior, just like you can little by little draw nearer to Him.** That is how Satan draws so many astray: he knows about this magical "little by little" principle and will use it to his benefit to make you think that the little steps you take in his direction aren't drastic enough to affect your eternal

progression.

Satan's Plan

If Satan is going to draw us away he is going to have an easier time doing it drawing us away little by little than by drastic changes. His teachings are "buy now, pay later", "have it all now", "instant gratification", "all or nothing" "never enough". This poverty, absolute, and lack mentality is a temporal mentality. In actuality the universe is abundant, there is always enough, abundance is an eternal mentality.

When our attitude changes to one of entitlement, pride, selfishness, and ungratefulness we are in grave danger! All of those attitudes put the self first and above everything else. How can you learn and grow if you are so focused on yourself that there is no room for outside influence? Every principle of the gospel is based on service. Service is the exact opposite of these dangerous attitudes. But it is Satan's plan to distract us from service and growth by placing the focus on ourselves.

To keep our eyes focused on the world's view-- selfishness, limited time, "eat drink and be merry for tomorrow we die" is exactly what Satan wants us to do. Our lives here have a purpose, to grow and learn. All the distractions and attitudes Satan would have us have are meant to keep us from growing, learning, and remembering the love for our fellow man that we had in the preexistence.

Anger, pride, selfishness, jealousy, entitlement, ungratefulness, procrastination, and hate all create a dam for our spirits-- that is they are slowed from progression just as a dam slows water. When filled with these negative emotions and thoughts we are unable to feel or share the love of our Savior. We are unable to focus on anything else but these emotions; they consume our spirit, shrink our heart, and blacken our soul. To spend one minute in any of these negative emotions is a waste of a minute that we could have had for an abundance of love, success, acceptance, gratitude, and blessings beyond measure.

Not just "food" storage

Part of having food storage includes non-food items as well. Clothes, toiletries, cash, medicine, fuel, blankets, etc. When building your food storage there are 3 stages to prepare for:

1. Food & supplies only: this stage is basically if your family is struggling financially and you need to rely on your food storage to feed your family. Electricity, running water, and gas are all still available under this circumstance so the main priority here is to have enough food, toiletries, and cash on hand to sustain your family until times get better.

2. No power or water: this stage means that there's been something happen so that there is no power to your house, and no running water. This stage you will need to have everything you've prepared for in stage 1, including: water, propane & camping stoves or solar oven, flashlights, batteries, wood (if you have a fireplace), generator, fuel, and such items you would need if you had no power or running water.

3. Ultimate disaster: this is the stage we all hope never happens, but being prepared for it will give you a sense of security. This stage is if the worse scenario

happened- major disaster to your house, or having to evacuate or move. This stage includes all the items in the previous 2 stages, as well as: camping items such as tents, sleeping bags, etc. , 4wd truck, trailer, gas, tools, and any other items your family would need if you had to pick up and live in nature.

Keeping these 3 stages in mind helps keep your focus on your food storage needs. There is no need to prepare for stage 3 if you don't have everything for stage 1 yet. As you are prepared for each stage you can start working on the next stage.

Medical Needs

If you have prescription medicines such as diabetic, prescription glasses or contacts, or other prescription products it's important to have some on hand for an emergency. Some medicines are illegal or almost impossible to get a supply of more than one month because of cost or government control; for those there's not much you can do. But having an extra pair of glasses, or buying your contacts in a 1-year supply is possible. Don't forget the contact solution!

Over-the-counter medicines are good to have as well. These medicines are good to rotate as they have an expiration date and can get stronger or weaker with time. The last thing you need in an emergency situation is a medicine overdose from an expired product. Which brings to point ipecac is a good thing to include in your food storage. Ipecac will make someone throw up and is useful in an emergency situation where overdose may have happened. Activated Charcoal is another useful item to have-- it helps with poison ingestion. If possible call the poison control first. These are only suggested to be used only as a back-up when no other options are available.

A good first-aid kit should be part of your house, food storage or not. More than just a few band-aids it should include things such as: rubbing alcohol, hydrogen peroxide, bandages, gauze, tweezers, tape, burn ointment, cleansing wipes, and scissors. You can purchase basic and advanced first aid-kits for under $20 and they are worth having.

Attending a basic first-aid class is also a good idea to learn how to take care of basic injuries, as well as what to do in a medical emergency. There are also medical emergency books that explain signs, symptoms and what you should do for illnesses. A resource like this could prove invaluable in an emergency situation.

Clothes

Clothes are only necessary to have in your food storage only for stage 3. However, you can still save money by purchasing clothes in the off-seasons for the next year. In the Spring for example you can usually find Fall and Winter clothes at extreme discounts. Usually for kids you can guess the size they will be in when the season comes around, and for adults it's even easier since the sizes don't change as drastically.

If you are going to purchase some clothes for 72-hour kits or food storage keep to basic durable clothing such as jeans & t-shirts, or overalls. Aside from never being out of style, jeans are also very durable and work for cold or warm weather. If there does come a time that you or your children need to wear them you more than likely won't care about name brand or designer clothes at that point.

If you know how to sew, fabric is also a good thing to have on hand for blankets, clothes, or any other needs that may arise. You don't need anything expensive or fancy. Bolts of fabric can be found pretty cheap when on clearance and one bolt would store pretty easily and still provide plenty of fabric for any needs. Sheets also make great fabric for sewing projects and can be just a few dollars each. In an emergency fabric can also be used as bandages for medical needs. If you are going to store fabric for making clothes and things, don't forget to store needles, thread, extra needles for your sewing machine, a good pair of scissors etc.

When my oldest was 3 months old almost overnight she outgrew most of her clothes. As new parents we were unprepared for this and had hardly anything for the next size. In an unforeseen shopping trip for clothes at a cheap department store we ended up paying $80 and got 5 onesies, 3 outfits, and 3 pair of pajamas. Boy did I learn my lesson! After that experience I started to buy clothes during the off-season and by the time our oldest reached her 18-month-old growth spurt I pulled out an entire wardrobe I had purchased months before during the off-season. When I totaled the price tags of the wardrobe it totaled almost $350. However, buying them all on off-season clearance I had paid only $60! I was converted to off-season buying! Off-season shopping does require a little bit of space to store the clothes until they are ready to be worn. If you are well organized you can keep them in bins or hung up in your child's closet until they'll fit.

Cash

It is important to have cash included in your food storage. If you are unable to go to the bank to get money, or have a financial struggle having enough cash in your food storage to provide for your family's needs for a few months could be a life saver.

Money can be saved for food storage in many different ways that won't require a drastic financial burden. Here are some ways I have tried:

1. Each time you are at the store take out $20 extra when checking out with your debit card. Especially after pay day this $20 may not make a big difference at the time, but when added to your food storage cash it will add up quickly.

2. Save your change. At the end of each day place any change into a jar or piggy bank. Make a habit to never use change when at the store-- always break a dollar so you get more change. Your change will add up and can be taken to the bank and totaled then given the dollar amount. Because of space you will probably want to store the dollars rather than the change.

3. Create a way to earn a small amount of money for the sole purpose of food storage cash. Have a yard or bake sale, sell things on ebay, clean houses, etc. When it's a

small job or task that can be done occasionally for one specific purpose it can be fun and exciting to do.

4. There is also the basic savings plan where you put aside 10% of each pay check towards your food storage cash.

You might also want to consider adding gold and silver to your food storage. The value of the dollar could drastically change, but gold and silver usually stay steadier.

With all of these it takes discipline to follow through and keep the money set aside for its purpose.

Important Documents

Originals or even copies of important documents such as birth certificates, passports, social-security cards, wills, titles, and so on are important to have in a safe place. Fire and water-proof document safes can be purchased reasonably cheaply and provide a safe place to keep your important documents and cash for emergencies.

If you have more than just a few important documents a larger safe may be necessary-- for instance if you want to protect family heirloom jewelry, journals, photo albums, or even to keep guns safe from children.

Keeping a photo id as well as an emergency credit or debit card in 72 hour kits are also a good idea. Just make sure that you replace the credit or debit card as it expires.

For those important documents that you use regularly and are not practical to keep in a safe, make copies and keep the copies in the safe. Driver's License, credit cards, Social Security cards etc would be examples of things to keep a copy of in a safe.

Weapons & Tools

Mostly for stage 3 food storage which hopefully never happens. But it is important to be able to protect your family from harm be it animal or human. Protection as well as possibly survival makes having a gun and ammunition necessary. Aside from guns there are other weapons that could come in handy such as a knife. Knives are considered a weapon, but have many more uses that could come in handy in an emergency situation. An axe is another example of something that can come in handy if wood is needed for a fire.

If you are anti-gun or weapon a suggested alternative would be a paintball gun. Paintball guns do not cause fatal injuries, but the sting of getting hit might deter an unwanted animal or human intruder. Paint balls are made from fish oil and are biodegradable if you are concerned about environmental issues. Paint balls do expire however so if you are going to store one make sure you check the expiration dates. A pellet gun or air soft gun might be another alternative.

A standard tool box of miscellaneous tools is a good idea to have. Most households probably already have a basic tool set including: hammer, screwdrivers, nails, screws, duct tape, and maybe even some more advanced tools such as a cordless drill, level, tape measure, etc. Years ago I purchased a box full of a variety of different nails and screws in different sizes; it has come in handy around the house and would be a great addition to food storage preparedness.

Duct tape is another staple. I've heard people jokingly say all you ever need is duct tape and a hammer, if one doesn't fix something the other will. WD-40 would also be a good item to have with your tools

Different widths of rope can also come in handy. For use as tie-downs, animal leads , clothes-line, tent supports and other needs.

Building your food storage

Let's face it, not many people can afford to just go out and purchase a couple thousand dollars of food storage at once. So for those of us that don't have an extra couple of thousand dollars lying around the best way to build our food storage is slowly and little by little.

These are some ways you can build your food storage without breaking your piggy bank.

1. Watch for the case-lot sales!

    a. Although you do need a little extra grocery money to purchase case-lots, you don't have to buy EVERYTHING all at once. Each time a case-lot sale is available purchase 1, 2, 5, or as many cases as you can afford of the items your family uses regularly.

    b. Store sales usually have a 12 week rotation- meaning an item will be on a good sale price ever 12 weeks, that means they will probably have a case-lot sale every 12 weeks as well. Knowing this you can plan your purchases according to what you will use for the next 12 weeks, as well as what you want to stock up on for food storage.

    c.   If there are items that aren't typically in case-lot sales, or that you see on a really good sale. A good rule of thumb is to purchase 12 weeks or more worth of that product (if possible) each time it comes on a good sale and you will never pay full price for the product again!

2. Buy a little extra each time you go to the store

    a.   If there are no case-lot sales coming up, or you don't have the extra money to buy them you can still build your food storage by just buying a little extra of the things already on your grocery list.

    b.   When at the grocery store, if you need 1 can of corn, buy 2-3 instead. When you do this with a few of your items on your list it will only add a few dollars onto your grocery bill, yet will add up in your cupboards!

    c.   When buying groceries regularly you won't miss the extra few dollars each time you're at the store, yet the extra items will build up your food storage before you know it! This can also be adapted to as much or as little as you can afford at the time. If it's only $1 extra each time you go to the store that's better than nothing.

3. Don't stop going to the store because you still have food in your cupboards!

    a. As you're building up your food storage the last thing you want to do is use it all up before you go grocery shopping again.

    b. For my grocery shopping I like to make a list of 10 meals each week, I purchase the ingredients for those 10 meals, then when I shop again in 7 days I will most-likely still have the ingredients for 2-3 meals. As long as they're not fresh foods it is a great way to build your food storage and make sure you have things to make complete meals in it.

4. Have a place to put your food storage

    a. Putting the extra food & supplies in a separate area of your house will allow you to build up a supply and will help you keep on your regular grocery shopping schedule as the things in your kitchen are used.

    b. You don't need a whole room, or even an entire closet, to store your food storage when you're starting out. You can start by even just allocating a shelf in a closet, under a bed, etc.

5. Make a list of the consumable items your family uses
    regularly (see our list example in this book)

    a. Add a few items to your grocery list when you
        go shopping

    b. Keep a tally on the items you have and the items
        you need to build up- that way you wont end up
        with a 5 year supply of shampoo and a 1 month
        supply of ketchup!

6. Rotate the food as you build your food storage.

    a. When you're purchasing your weekly groceries
        put new purchased items behind old ones in
        your food storage. That way you use the oldest
        ones first and nothing will spoil.

    b. Rotating your food storage will also make sure
        that your family is using and likes the items you
        have, and that their digestive system and taste
        buds is used to it too.

7. Purchase the brands and products your family likes.

    a. If your family loves Heinz Ketchup, but Hunts is
        on sale, don't buy it!! Most-likely no one will
        want to eat it, or they will complain when they
        do. It's a waste of money to buy food storage
        items your family wont eat or doesn't like.

b. It will also seem like less of an adjustment if your food storage consists of food items you already eat regularly. Let's face it, no one wants to go from eating a nice variety of meals to meals of just beans and rice…. And if you have children it's not worth the complaining you would hear either.

Where do I store it all?

For some people they use the excuse of not having enough room to store everything. Well let me just tell you- I have lived in a 3-bedroom 2 bathroom house with probably less than 1,300 square feet, and 6 of us living there and having TONS of stuff I use for the different projects such as sewing, scrapbooking, and crafts I do regularly. Any of you who do those things understand it takes some room to store those things. Not to mention the basic holiday decorations, books, cooking gadgets, baby items, and other things most people have in their house for occasional use. To make matters worse we didn't have a garage to help lighten the burden of "seasonal stuff" in the house. Yet with all this, we had food storage!

Where did we put it? Everywhere I could!

Under the bed in the boys room was the holding place for all our #10 cans full of wheat, rice, beans, flour, sugar, and dehydrated or freeze-dried items such as eggs, cheese powder, sour cream powder, corn, apple slices, peas & carrots, celery, powdered milk, and any other items of the sort I could get my hands on. Needless to say under the entire twin size bed was full of cans and cases of cans. (which also meant kids couldn't hid messes under the bed) I fit the cans in a 6x12 rectangle holding a grand total of 72 cans! They were out of the way, no one even knew they were there, and they were going into a space that usually just ends up being trash and mess from kids shoving stuff under it anyway.

My kids had a dresser in their rooms- one in each room that held all their clothes. Since their clothes are in dressers their closets were free for storage! The boy's closet was half holiday storage, and half food storage with a long shelf we put in the top to hold extra blankets, suitcases, and some baby items. I purchased a standalone shelf unit for under $40 that fit inside their closet and held canned meats (tuna), soups such as tomato & cream of chicken soup, as well as large bags of sugar and flour- foods we uses more regularly. On top of a taller chest of drawers in the boy's room I stacked canned veggies we use more often- green beans, corn, mushrooms, etc. since my boys were too short at the time to be able to keep stuff on top of the dresser.

In my daughters room the closet was purely food storage. We used 2 more of the shelf units that could stack as high or low as I wanted to hold the items in her closet, along with some shelves we put up high. Her closet held canned fruits, baking items, cereal, seasonings, and all the other food items we used on a regular basis. We had room under her bed for some #10 cans, and so we started to fill in that space as well. (that is something we've built up and continue to build up little by little- buying a few cans here and there)

What about non-food storage items?

That house did not have a hall closet (to store towels/sheets etc. in) so I put another one of the shelf units at the end of the hall. Using the top shelf from the two units in my daughter's closet I made the hall shelf unit 2 shelves taller. This shelf unit held our towels, pillow cases, bottles of things I had canned, extra bar soap, extra Kleenex, and our toilet paper storage.

I kept extra cleaning supplies and laundry soap items on the shelf above the washer and dryer (which was is in our hallway at the time- so if you have a separate laundry room, count yourself lucky!). Extra dishwasher soap was kept under the kitchen sink. Extra shampoo & conditioner were stored under the bathroom sink.

Medicines, hydrogen peroxide, band-aids, feminine hygiene products, rubbing alcohol and other such items we kept either under the master bathroom sink, or in an over-the-door shoe organizer on one of the doors.

Oh and did I mention that most of the time living in that house I was also a single mom to 4 kids? So not only was space limited, but finances as well.

If we could build food storage in that tiny house, and with my limited budget at the time, anyone can! Over the years we have lived in larger houses, some having more food storage space than others, but we're not going to let house size stop us from building our food storage!

Basic Food Storage System

For those new to food storage or those that may be lacking in cooking skills here is an easy way to get your food storage in a basic, simple way that won't overwhelm you!

Start Small

For this example I will be only be referring to the dinner meal when I say "meal"

1. Pick 10 meals that your family enjoys. 10 is a good number because that gives you a little variety, so you're not stuck with the same 7 meals each week.
2. Make a list of each item required to make each of the 10 meals.
3. Combine repeat ingredients (so if you need 1 can of corn for one meal, and 1 can for another meal, total you need 2 cans of corn for the 10 meals).
4. Now, multiply the list by the amount of food storage you want! For a 1-month supply multiply your list by 3. Or you can do what I do which is always overestimate, so for my 10-meals I might say they equal 1 week (which gives us either 3 extra meals, or 3 nice lunches). So I

would multiply the 10-meal list by 4 to have a one-month supply.

You now have your shopping list for a one month supply of meals. (Dinner meals)

Use this same formula for more meals, as well as a longer supply.

Once you have your meals picked out it's easy to build up your food storage little by little!

This is a good system for those just getting started with food storage, or those that do not do a lot of cooking from scratch, and even those who are OCD when it comes to exactness.

Start now to get your family used to food storage meals

For those whose families live off processed, pre-made, or fast food it's time to make some small changes! Fast food may not be available to get some day. Make little changes now to enable you to have and love the food you can store. Start with once a week that you make a meal with all ingredients you can add to your food storage. Spaghetti is a great and easy one to start with because you can store bottled spaghetti sauce, and noodles. Some premade and processed foods such as canned soups, boxed meals, mac & cheese etc. can be a great addition to food storage-- you just have to be aware of the expiration dates on them.

I've often wondered-- we've become such a spoiled society with so much waste that if it came down to living off food storage how many people will starve rather than eat something basic and non-processed they are not used to? We're used to fast food; pizza, frozen dinners, and the convenience of getting what you want now, and having it taste great. What happens when people actually have to make their own food, and it's not going to taste like the restaurant food they're used to? Have you ever been guilty of skipping meals because nothing "sounds good"? That is evidence of our spoiled upbringing! It's a mentality, and we let our brain determine what and if we are going to eat rather than giving our body what it needs to survive.

Make small changes and efforts to have at least 10 meals that your family will eat and you can store the ingredients in your food storage. Even if you are resorting to canned ravioli, rice-a-roni, mac & cheese, spaghetti, ramen noodles, spaghetti-o's, tuna helper, and other easily stored items. Just be aware the nutrient content of these aren't the best and the processing isn't as healthy as other food choices. But if it's all you know your family will eat, it's a start!

Make sure to include some canned fruits and veggies for the nutritional value to include with your meals, or better yet, use freeze dried foods (such as Thrive Life) in both daily use as well as for your food storage since they often have a higher nutritional value than even fresh foods.

Storing perishable Foods

Remember that some meals require milk, eggs, or other ingredients that may not be available if you are living off your food storage. Powdered milk is great to have on hand, and although some don't care for the taste, if it is needed in one of your favorite recipes you'll be glad you have it! You can also buy shelf-stable milk, cream, and even chocolate milk. Gossner Cheese Company makes some. You can see their products at www.gossner.com

Cheese, sour cream, buttermilk, eggs, whipping cream, and butter can all be bought in a powder form as well. Again, they might be a good thing to have on hand just in case there are no other options. You can purchase these types of powdered items from Thrive Life at: www.what8ate.thrivelife.com .

 You can bottle butter- Wendy Dewitt[1] explains how to bottle butter in her video "Everything under the sun" you can view it at http://www.youtube.com/watch?v=HhGaTlwYs-s

Cheese can be frozen if it is shredded first. There are also freeze dried options for cheese from Thrive Life at www.what8ate.thrivelife.com

---

[1] See references page for Wendy's blog for more information

Eggs can be stored for up to a year, all you have to do is wipe each egg with mineral oil, then put them back into the fridge. The easiest way we have found to do this is to put on a plastic glove and dip your fingers into a bowl of mineral oil, and then rub them over the egg until it has a good coating. Always crack eggs into a separate container to be on the safe side. If an egg has gone bad you will smell it. You can also use an egg substitute for recipes.

Egg Substitute for 1 egg:

- 1 t. unflavored gelatin
- 2 T. boiling water
- 2 T. cold water

Whisk gelatin in boiling water to dissolve. Add cold water. Use in baking instead of eggs. Multiply

recipe for more than one egg.

When it comes to fresh fruits you can slice and freeze them, dry them, or bottle them. Some fruits do not handle bottling such as bananas and strawberries, but if you love them as much as my family does you'll defiantly want to have some in your food storage. Dehydrating them is one option using a food dryer, and then you can seal them in a vacuum-packed jar or bag. Freezing them keeps a fresher taste; however you need freezer space and the hopes that you will always have electricity.

Vacuum-Packing

Using a vacuum sealer such as a food saver with a jar-sealing attachment is a great way to store some of your shelf-stable but short-expiration items. Chocolate, for example, turns white and loses flavor and texture in a matter of 6 months or so. By placing chocolate chips or chocolate candies into a glass jar, then vacuum-sealing it you make it shelf-stable for years at the same quality. This can be done for any shelf-stable items you are concerned about expiration dates with: cakes, stuffing mix, bread crumbs, muffin mix, candy, licorice, dried fruit, jerky, and so on.

Any item that you want to vacuum-pack that is a powder-- make sure you put it or keep it in a bag inside the jar so you don't suck up the powder into your vacuum machine. Buying candy and chocolate after the holidays when they are on clearance really cheap then vacuuming them is a great way to add a little sweet stuff to your food storage without breaking your bank account!

When vacuum-packing items in jars, wide-mouth jars are easier to fill and empty when you are packing unusual shaped or bulky items. The great thing about vacuum-sealing jars is you can reuse the lid. If you have a jar of jerky, for example, you can open the jar, take out what you want, and then reseal it. The lids do not have to be boiled either.

Food-saver vacuums can be purchased in the stores, or even more cheaply online. The stores sell them for about $80-100, but you can get them online for less than $50 on ebay. I have found the jar-sealing attachments for both regular-size lids and wide-mouth jar lids on ebay for under $10 each.

Think of all the awesome things you can store in vacuum-sealed jars! See's chocolates (or any other deluxe name brand you like), fruit snacks (for kids), jelly beans, starbursts, m&m's, skittles, jerky, nuts, trail mix, cookies, brownie or cake mix, and more! This turns average food storage into a luxurious one!

How to vacuum-seal a jar:

- Place the desired objects into your jar. (DO NOT vacuum a jar with only powder! If you want to vacuum-pack a powdered mix or item, place that item in a Ziploc bag, then inside the jar. Otherwise you could get the powder dust up in your food saver and cause problems).
- Place the seal only (no ring) on the jar.
- Cover the seal with your food-saver jar-sealer attachment. You will need the right-size; wide-mouth attachment cannot do regular jars for example.

- Insert the hose into the top of the attachment, and the other end of the hose into the food saver.
- Press the food saver down (where you would normally have the bag coming out of); hold it down for 3 seconds or so and when you let up the machine will continue to run. It will stop itself when it's done.
- Once it's stopped itself, remove the hose from the attachment.
- Remove the attachment from the seal.
- Your jar should now be sealed and you can screw on the ring.

Using a food saver to vacuum-seal jars you can reuse the seals. Simply open the jar, remove how much you want, then reseal it like above using the same seal. This aspect is really nice because when you have items in the jar you may not use all the contents of such as candy, nuts, jerky etc.

Tools for Preparing Foods

Having food may not mean much if you don't have the tools you need to prepare them! Here is as list of some basic recommended items to make sure are in your food storage:

- Baking pans
- Can opener
- Knife
- Matches or lighter
- Mixing bowl
- Plates
- Scissors
- Spatula & other cooking utensils
- Utensils

Some other tools that would be a good idea to have are:

- Dutch ovens with charcoal & any other accessories
- Pressure canner/cooker[1]
- Solar oven and/or camping stove[2]

---

[1] Make sure your pressure gauge has been checked if you move to a different altitude

[2] Costco has had a mini camping oven and stove for around $150 that runs off propane and would be perfect!

- Solar powered items such as a radio, flashlight, and charger for devices (I am a BIG fan of solar powered stuff- we even have solar powered Christmas lights!)
- Water bath canner & tools to can foods

You can also make your own solar oven using cardboard boxes and tinfoil. Here are instructions on how to make your own solar oven from ehow.com:

DIY Solar Oven Instructions

Things You'll Need

- Aluminum Foil
- Cardboard
- Large And Small Cardboard Boxes
- Non-toxic Glues
- Non-toxic Invisible Tape
- Plastic Wrap
- Scissors
- Newspaper
- Pencils
- Black Construction Paper
- Staplers

1. Find two boxes. One should fit inside the other with a 2- to 3-inch space on each side. (This can vary slightly - the space will be filled with newspaper.)
2. Line the bottom of the large box with crumpled newspaper.
3. Place the smaller box inside the large box.
4. Fill the space between the sides of the two boxes with crumpled newspaper.

5. Line the sides of the inside of the smaller box with aluminum foil. You can use a non-toxic tape or fold the edges of foil over the top of the box to hold it in place.

6. Line the bottom of the inside of the smaller box with black construction paper to absorb heat.

7. Lay a piece of cardboard on top of the large box and trace the shape of the box onto the cardboard.

8. Add 2 inches around the trace line and cut out to make a reflector.

9. Cover the cardboard piece with aluminum foil. Smooth out any wrinkles and secure the aluminum foil to the cardboard with non-toxic glue or tape.

10. Staple the reflector to the outside back of the large box.

11. Situate the oven with the box opening up and the reflector facing the sun for maximum heat.

12. Place food to be cooked in the solar oven. (See "How to Use a Solar Oven," under Related eHows.)

13. Stretch clear plastic wrap across the top of the large box. Secure the plastic with tape around the entire box.

How to use your solar oven[1]

Instructions

Things You'll Need

- Solar Oven
- Glass, Cast Iron or ceramic Pot
- Food

1. Select your cooking pots carefully. While most solar ovens come with a cooking pot, they are not the only ones available to cook in. Glass, tin or cast iron pots and pans all work wonderfully well, containing heat and allowing temperatures to rise while cooking the food inside. Black pots and pans help to reduce cooking times and should be considered. Painting clear glass black on the outside is also a great time saver. Simply make sure you leave some part clear so you can see the food inside. Place a dark baking pan on the bottom of your oven to help catch any run over and keep your oven clean

2. Aim your solar oven properly. Your solar oven reflectors should be completely free from shadow. To accomplish this, adjust the cooker from the back, watching the front and checking for shadows on the sides. Place the cooker in front of the path of the sun, and it will receive the most sunlight for as long as possible before you have to make any further adjustments. Place a few rocks in front

---

[1] Instructions from ehow.com

and behind it to keep it from moving and to provide stability.

3. Place your food already in your chosen cooking container in the solar oven. Place the food that will take the longest to cook in first. Experiment with amounts and timings. Remember to allow for expansion as well. For example, beans and rice both expand as they are cooking, so you want to be sure to leave enough room at the top of your container to allow for this. Poking a small hole or leaving the container lid loose will help with any pressure buildup.

4. Place your items where it is hottest.

Time your meals. Remember, cooking with the solar oven takes time.

5. Place your items in the oven early in the day to allow for the most cooking time. Your foods will be basically "slow-cooked" so be prepared. Items that will need longer cooking should be in black containers and placed towards the back of the cooker where the heat will be greatest. Chicken, beans and carrots will take anywhere from 3 to 4 hours of cooking time. Checking your food is advisable, as long as it is done quickly and the containers are covered as soon as possible to prevent heat loss.

Every time you open a lid, it takes a little bit longer to warm up again.

Freezer Meals

Freezer meals are a great way to make dinners easy and quick for nights you don't have the time or energy to make a healthy meal. Whenever I make any type of casserole or large dish I almost always make 5x as much as we need for that meal and will put the extras into a freezer and oven-safe dish that I can freeze and bake on another day. It's just as easy to make a super large batch as it is one regular batch, and doesn't take too many more ingredients. Plus, if it's a meal that is a mess to make-- using a lot of pans etc. then you have to clean up the mess only once! You can purchase the ingredients in bulk and save money as well.

Each time I was pregnant I would stock up on freezer meals a month or two before I was due; it made post-baby life MUCH easier for a week or two. All I or my husband had to do was throw a freezer meal in the oven, and heat up some veggies or make a salad and dinner was done!

Some of the freezer meals I make regularly include:

- Lasagna
- Funeral potatoes
- Shepherd's pie

- Chicken pot pie

- Aussie chicken

- Meatloaf

- Chicken & Broccoli Casserole

- Veggie Lasagna

- Stroganoff

- Tater-Tot Casserole

You can purchase containers that can be frozen as well as baked in the oven at restaurant stores such as Smart & Final, or online at Amazon.com. Make sure to get the ones with baking lids-- not the clear plastic lids. When you finish your freezer meal be sure to label what it is, as well as the month/year if you're worried about it getting lost in the bottom of the freezer. Sometimes I also write cooking instructions on them for my husband, or someone I might give the meal to.

You can also get microwavable disposable containers- I've found some on Amazon that can even be put in the dishwasher and reused. These are great for lunches! You can see and purchase them here: https://amzn.to/2U6curk

Canning aka Bottling

Canning foods are a great way to preserve homemade and fresh foods and know exactly what's in them. Canning has been done for hundreds of years. With the harvest from the garden, food was then canned to be eaten in the winter and before the next harvest. Canning is a very simple process that anyone can learn to do! Here are some things you will need:

Bottles- they come in half pint, pint, and quart sizes and also include regular or wide mouth which refers to the circumference of the lid. Personally, I prefer wide mouth, especially if you're canning something large like peaches or pears or something you'll want to scoop out. But for things like salsa or applesauce regular mouth are fine.

Seals- these can only be used once (except for if you are vacuum packing)

Rings- tighten the seal onto the jar as its sealing. Once the jar is sealed the ring is not necessary and doesn't have to be stored on the jar

Canning pan with rack- These can be found at many stores, they are usually dark blue with white specks on them. The pan includes a lid, and a rack to hold the jars as they boil.

Jar grabber- this is used to grab the jars out of the boiling water and are very handy

Magnetic seal grabber- these are not necessary, but make canning much easier. You use the tip of this to grab the seals out of boiling water before putting them onto the jars to seal.

Funnel- a large opening funnel makes filling jars much easier and less messy.

*****If you are planning on bottling meats and/or vegetables you MUST have:**

Pressure canner/cooker- this is a special pan that must be used for meats and vegetables in order to get all the bacteria out in the sealing process.

There are a lot of great recipes for canning, one website I recently found contains a bunch of great looking recipes is: http://www.canning-recipes.com/

In the next section I have included step by step instructions on canning different types of foods, as well as a few recipes.

Bottled Meals

Another way to make homemade meals that you can store for food storage is bottled meals. These are great because they are shelf-stable and don't need to be kept in the freezer. Wendy Dewitt has even bottled cakes and breads, she tells/shows how in her video "what are you waiting for?" Her video and book "Everything under the Sun" are GREAT resources for bottling! You can do a youtube or google search for her name and find her website or videos easily.

When it comes to bottled meals, personally I stick to soups. Whenever I make a homemade Turkey or Ham soup it's great to bottle some! Because soups generally have veggies and/or meat in them they HAVE to be processed in a pressure canner/cooker. Process time is for the ingredient that has longest processing time in your manual that came with the pan. See charts in the bottling section.

Making a homemade Turkey or Ham soup is easy. After your meal, put the leftover meat and bones into a large pot, cover with water, add a generous amount of salt (it pulls the flavor out of the bones) and simmer on the lowest setting over night. (this makes clean up easy that night too) The next morning you will need to add water again. You can keep adding water until you are ready to make the soup. Then strain the juice (water that now has good flavor from the meat and bones), and sort through to separate the meat from the bones. (ham is really easy because there are usually just a couple large bones, turkey can be more time consuming with all the little bones) Add your meat to the juice along with any other vegetables you want such as carrots, potatoes, celery, corn, etc. Simmer until vegetables are cooked. Add seasonings if needed. If you want noodles wait until 30 minutes before serving to add them so they don't get soggy. <u>You don't want to bottle soup with noodles because they will get VERY soggy!</u> It's best to just bottle the soup without noodles, then when you open it if you want you can add noodles to it as it's used.

Bottling Meats & Vegetables

Bottling meats is a great way to have shelf stable meat in your food storage. You can bottle any meat. The meat will be cooked inside the bottle and makes a quick meal preparation when used. When you bottle meats you can pack them into the bottles cooked or raw-- depending on your preference. There is no need to add water to any jar of meat with the exception of ground meats. You can season the meat, but be careful to not over-season as the flavor will get stronger and sometimes bitter when bottled (such as garlic). Meat MUST be bottled in a pressure canner/cooker. Always use high-quality jars when bottling in a pressure canner/cooker and make sure you set the bottles on the rack inside the pan.

Bottling Chicken or Chunks of Meat

Chicken can be packed into the bottles raw or cooked. You can fit more chicken into the bottle if it's raw so that's what I do. Either way the chicken will be fully cooked when you are finished. There is no need to add water when bottling chicken. Be sure to pack the meat tight and still allow the ½" space at the top. The meat will shrink as you process it. Even when I pack my bottles tight, after processing they are about ¾ full.

1.   Pack chicken or meat into the bottles
2.   Add ¼- ½ teaspoon of salt
3.   Wipe the top of the bottle clean-- where the seal will go
4.   Boil the seals in water to soften them (good to do while filling the jars)
5.   Place a seal on each jar
6.   Screw the ring onto each jar
7.   Place into your pressure canner/cooker
8.   Fill the pressure canner/cooker with about 3-4" of water

Follow processing lbs. of pressure according to your altitude

Meat-processing time is 75 minutes for pints, and 90 minutes for quarts.

Bottling Ground Meat

Cook the ground meat just as if you were going to use it. Seasoning can be done but is optional. Some like to add taco seasoning for an easy taco night in the future. Some seasonings such as garlic can go bitter, so if you do season it add sparingly.

1. Fill each jar with the cooked meat
2. Cover with water until ½" from the top
3. Wipe the top of the bottle clean-- where the seal will go
4. Boil the seals in water to soften them (good to do while filling the jars)
5. Place a seal on each jar
6. Screw the ring onto each jar
7. Place into your pressure canner/cooker
8. Fill the pressure canner/cooker with about 3-4" of water

Follow processing lbs. of pressure according to your altitude

Meat-processing time is 75 minutes for pints, and 90 minutes for quarts.

Bottling Vegetables

Vegetables also have to be bottled in a pressure canner/cooker. They are a great way to store and use your garden veggies all year round. When you find a good deal on veggies, have lots from your bountiful basket, have or know someone with a plentiful garden, bottling is a great way to preserve them so they don't go to waste!

1. Prepare the veggies-- such as cut up, peel, etc.
2. Fill the jars with the veggies leaving ½" room at the top
3. Cover with water until ½" from the top
4. Wipe the top of the bottle clean-- where the seal will go
5. Boil the seals in water to soften them (good to do while filling the jars)
6. Place a seal on each jar
7. Screw the ring onto each jar
8. Place into your pressure canner/cooker
9. Fill the pressure canner/cooker with about 3-4" of water

Follow processing lbs. of pressure according to your altitude. Charts are usually provided when you purchase your canner or can be easily found online.

For vegetables see this chart from:

http://www.livingoffgrid.org/pressure-canning-chart-foods-processing-times-psi-and-elevation/

Pressure Canning Chart							
This canning chart shows processing times for low-acid foods, which **must** be canned using a pressure canner. The processing times below are for canning at sea level using a weighted-gauge pressure canner. For more foods and canning guidelines see Ball Blue Book of Canning.							
		Process Time		**PSI** (*pounds per square inch*)			
Food	**Pack Method**	Pints	Quarts	- 2000 ft.	2001- 4000 ft.	4001- 6000 ft.	6001- 8000 ft.
Artichokes (Jerusalem)	Hot	25 min.	25 min.	11 lb.	12 lb.	13 lb.	14 lb.
Asparagus	Raw Hot	30 min. 30 min.	40 min. 40 min.	11 lb. 11 lb.	12 lb. 12 lb.	13 lb. 13 lb.	14 lb. 14 lb.
Beans (green or yellow)	Raw Hot	20 min. 20 min.	25 min. 25 min.	11 lb. 11 lb.	12 lb. 12 lb.	13 lb. 13 lb.	14 lb. 14 lb.
Beets	Hot	30 min.	35 min.	11 lb.	12 lb.	13 lb.	14 lb.

Broccoli	Canning is not recommended. Best to freeze or pickle for preservation.						
Brussels Sprouts	Canning is not recommended. Best to freeze or pickle for preservation.						
Cabbage	Canning is not recommended. Best kept in cold storage.						
Carrots	Raw Hot	25 min. 25 min.	30 min. 30 min.	11 lb. 11 lb.	12 lb. 12 lb.	13 lb. 13 lb.	14 lb. 14 lb.
Cauliflower	Canning is not recommended. Best to freeze for preservation.						
Corn	Raw Hot	55 min. 55 min.	85 min. 85 min.	11 lb. 11 lb.	12 lb. 12 lb.	13 lb. 13 lb.	14 lb. 14 lb.
Eggplant	Canning is not recommended.						
Lima Beans	Raw Hot	40 min. 40 min.	50 min. 50 min.	11 lb. 11 lb.	12 lb. 12 lb.	13 lb. 13 lb.	14 lb. 14 lb.
Mushrooms	Hot	45 min.		11 lb.	12 lb.	13 lb.	14 lb.
Okra	Raw Hot	25 min. 25 min.	40 min. 40 min.	11 lb. 11 lb.	12 lb. 12 lb.	13 lb. 13 lb.	14 lb. 14 lb.
Peas	Raw Hot	40 min. 40 min.	40 min. 40 min.	11 lb. 11 lb.	12 lb. 12 lb.	13 lb. 13 lb.	14 lb. 14 lb.
Peas (snap)	Canning is not recommended. Best to freeze for preservation.						

Peppers	Hot	35 min.		11 lb.	12 lb.	13 lb.	14 lb.
Potatoes, White	Hot	35 min.	40 min.	11 lb.	12 lb.	13 lb.	14 lb.
Pumpkin	Hot	55 min.	90 min.	11 lb.	12 lb.	13 lb.	14 lb.
Spinach and Other Greens	Hot	70 min.	90 min.	11 lb.	12 lb.	13 lb.	14 lb.
Squash (summer)	Canning is not recommended. Best eaten fresh.						
Squash (winter)	Hot	55 min.	90 min.	11 lb.	12 lb.	13 lb.	14 lb.
Sweet Potatoes	Hot	65 min.	90 min.	11 lb.	12 lb.	13 lb.	14 lb.

Bottling Fruits & Jams

Fruits and jams are easy to bottle and need only to be processed in a water bath which takes far less time to process. When canning fruit you want to fill the jar to 1/2" from the top with syrup (made of sugar and water) after you fill the jar with fruit.

If making a freezer jam:

1. Remove any stems, blanch, & peel if necessary
2. Slice if large
3. In a large bowl use a potato masher (or even a food processer for more fine jam)
4. Add sugar-- usually twice as much sugar as fruit
5. Stir well and let sit for at least 10 minutes
6. Boil pectin according to directions inside the box
7. Add pectin to fruit & sugar mixture
8. Mix well, then fill jars leaving ½" from the top
9. Wipe the top of the bottle clean-- where the seal will go
10. Boil the seals in water to soften them (good to do while filling the jars)
11. Place a seal on each jar
12. Screw the ring onto each jar
13. Keep in the freezer

Strawberry Freezer Jam

- 2 c. crushed strawberries

- 2 T. lemon juice

- 4 c. sugar

Mix and let sit for 10 minutes.

Combine separately:

- ¾ c. water

- 1 box pectin

Bring to full rolling boil. Boil hard for 1 minute stirring

constantly.

Add to fruit mixture. Mix for 3 minutes.

Ladle into jars leaving ½" at the top. Apply caps and let set-- no

longer than 24 hours before freezing.

If making a shelf-stable jam:

1. If necessary: blanch, peel and slice fruit

2. In a large pan combine fruit with twice as much sugar

3. Cook on Medium until fruit is very soft

4. Mash with a potato masher or puree in food processer

   for fine jam

5. Add pectin to boiling fruit & sugar

6. After 2 minutes remove from heat

7. Pour into jars leaving ½" from the top

8. Wipe the top of the bottle clean-- where the seal will go

9. Boil the seals in water to soften them (good to do while filling the jars)

10. Place a seal on each jar

11. Screw the ring onto each jar

12. Place in water-bath canner

13. Fill water to 1" above the jars

14. Process for time according to fruit and altitude

15. Processing time starts once water is at a full boil

Peach Mango Jam

- 10-14 peaches

- 5 mangos

Boil peaches and mangos whole in water for a couple minutes, and then transfer immediately to cold water. The skins should come off easily. Cut up both into chunks. Blend in food processor until desired consistency.

- Cook with 4-5 c. sugar, and 1 box pectin.

Bring to a boil and boil for 2 minutes. Fill jars and process in a water bath for 20 minutes (processing time is for my elevation of 5,000 feet).

Pear Jam (this is my grandma's famous recipe)

- 4 cups finely chopped pears(3 ½ lbs)
- 1 pkg pectin
- ¼ cup lemon juice
- ¼ pkg strawberry jello
- 6 cups sugar

DO NOT DOUBLE RECIPE. IT WILL NOT FIT IN STOCK POT

1. Bring boiling water canner, half-full with water, to simmer.

2. Wash jars and screw bands in hot, soapy water; rinse with warm water. Pour boiling water over flat lids in saucepan off the heat. Let stand in water until ready to use. Drain well before filling.

3. Measure EXACT amount of prepared pears into 8-qt. stock pot. Stir in lemon juice.

Measure EXACT amount of sugar into separate bowl.

Stir in 1 box pectin and ¼ box strawberry jello into fruit in saucepan.

6. Bring mixture to full rolling boil on high heat, stirring constantly.

7. Stir in sugar quickly. Return to full rolling boil and boil exactly 4 minutes stirring constantly. Remove from heat. Skim off any foam with metal spoon.

Ladle quickly into prepared jars, filling to within 1/8 inch of tops. Wipe jar rims and threads. Cover with two-piece lids. Screw bands tightly. Place jars in water bath. Water must cover jars by 1 to 2 inches; Cover-- then bring to a gentle boil. Process jars for 10 minutes (add 10 more minutes if you live in Cedar City). Adjust to your altitude if necessary. Check the pectin insert for processing times. Remove jars and place upright on a towel to cool completely. After jars cool, check seals by pressing middle of lid with finger. (If lid springs back, lid is not sealed and refrigeration is needed.)
Store unopened jam in a cool dark place up to 1 year. Refrigerate opened jams up to 3 weeks.

YIELD: 7 jelly jars per batch

Bottling whole or sliced fruit

If the fruit is soft and has a skin to be removed (such as peaches):

1. Blanch the fruit to soften it
2. Place into cold water and the skin should remove easily
3. Remove pits or seeds if necessary
4. Slice and fill jars
5. Fill to ½" from the top with syrup
1. Wipe the top of the bottle clean-- where the seal will go
2. Boil the seals in water to soften them (good to do while filling the jars)
3. Place a seal on each jar
4. Screw the ring onto each jar
5. Place into your water-bath canner
6. Fill the water bath canner with enough water until about 1" over the top of the jars
7. Processing time starts once water is at a full boil
8. Process for time according to the fruit and your altitude

If the fruit is hard with a skin (such as apples):

1. Use a peeler-corer-slicer

2. Cut in half if desired

3. Fill jars

4. Fill to ½" from the top with syrup

5. Wipe the top of the bottle clean-- where the seal will go

6. Boil the seals in water to soften them (good to do while filling the jars)

7. Place a seal on each jar

8. Screw the ring onto each jar

9. Place into your water-bath canner

10. Fill the water bath canner with enough water until about 1" over the top of the jars

11. Processing time starts once water is at a full boil

12. Process for time according to the fruit and your altitude

How to make syrup:

http://www.gopresto.com/recipes/canning/fruits.php

Heat sugar with water or juice until sugar is dissolved. Add fruit and cook until heated through. Pack fruit into clean Mason jars to within 1/2-inch of top of jar. Cover with hot liquid leaving 1/2-inch headspace. The liquid may be syrup, fruit juice, or plain water.

SYRUPS FOR CANNING FRUITS

SYRUP	SUGAR PER QUART OF LIQUID	YIELD OF SYRUP
Very Light	1 cup	4 1/2 cup
Light	2 cups	5 cups
Medium	3 cups	5 1/2 cups
Heavy	4 3/4 cups	6 1/2 cups

Applesauce

The easiest way to make applesauce is by having a hand crank or machine that separates the core, skin and apple. I use an attachment on my Kitchen Aid which saves muscle & energy! My mom has a hand crank one that works, but it is work! They both have the same result-- you put the cooked apples into one end and it separates the applesauce from the peel, seeds, and core at the other end. If you don't have either machine it is possible to still make applesauce by using a peeler-corer-slicer, cooking the slices, and then pureeing them in a food processer (or potato masher if you're REALLY motivated and lacking tools)

1. Cut apples into quarters

2. Boil until soft

3. Place quarters into your applesauce machine (hand crank or electric)

4. You can flavor the applesauce to your taste with sugar, cinnamon, etc. (optional)

5. Spoon applesauce into jars leaving ½" from the top

6. Wipe the top of the bottle clean-- where the seal will go

7. Boil the seals in water to soften them (good to do while filling the jars)

8. Place a seal on each jar

9. Screw the ring onto each jar

10. Place into your water-bath canner

11. Fill the water bath canner with enough water until about 1" over the top of the jars

12. Processing time starts once water is at a full boil

13. Process for time according to the fruit and your altitude

When you are bottling, altitude plays a large role:

ALTITUDE CHART FOR BOILING WATER CANNING FRUITS AND TOMATOES

ALTITUDE	PINTS AND QUARTS
1,001 – 3,000 ft.	Increase processing time 5 minutes
3,001 – 6,000 ft.	Increase processing time 10 minutes
6,001 – 8,000 ft.	Increase processing time 15 minutes

For processing times see this chart from--

http://www.recipetips.com/kitchen-tips/t--1396/canning-temperatures-and-processing-times.asp

High Acid Foods - Boiling-Water-Bath Canning Method			
Headspace: Leave 1/2 inch headspace on all high acid foods with two exceptions. When canning strawberry jam - leave 1/4 inch headspace. When canning grapes - leave 1 inch headspace.			

Food Type	Pack Method	Process Time - Minutes	
		Pint Jars	Quart Jars
Apples	Hot	20	20
Apricots	Raw Hot	25 20	30 25
Blackberries	Raw Hot	15 15	20 15
Blueberries	Raw Hot	15 15	20 15
Cranberries	Hot	15	15
Cherries	Raw Hot	25 15	30 20
Cucumbers (pickled in vinegar brine)	Raw	10	15
Grapefruit	Raw	10	10
Grapes	Raw Hot	15 10	20 10

Nectarines	Raw Hot	25 20	30 25
Oranges	Raw	10	10
Peaches	Raw Hot	25 20	30 25
Pears	Raw Hot	25 20	30 25
Plums	Raw Hot	20 25	20 25
Raspberries	Raw Hot	15 15	20 15
Rhubarb	Hot	15	15
Strawberry Jam	Hot	5	
Pineapple	Hot	15	20
Tomatoes - Juice (with acid added)	Hot	35	40
Tomatoes - Whole or halved - No Liquid Added (with acid added)	Raw	85	85
Tomatoes - Crushed (Quartered) - No Liquid Added (with acid added)	Hot	35	45

High Altitude:

The processing times above are for canning at sea level. Adjust as shown below:

Processing Time at Sea Level	Adjusted Processing Time
20 Minutes or Less	Add 1 minute per 1000 ft. in elevation
Over 20 Minutes	Add 2 minutes per 1000 ft. in elevation.

Freeze-Dried foods

Freeze-dried foods are another great item to have in your food storage. Usually purchased in pantry size or #10 cans these foods are the best option for shelf life, color retention, quality of nutrients and flavor, and easy to store. The process of freeze-drying[1] foods is:

1. Freezing: The product is frozen. This provides a necessary condition for low temperature drying.

2. Vacuum: After freezing, the product is placed under vacuum. This enables the frozen solvent in the product to vaporize without passing through the liquid phase, a process known as sublimation.

3. Heat: Heat is applied to the frozen product to accelerate sublimation.

4. Condensation: Low-temperature condenser plates remove the vaporized solvent from the vacuum chamber by converting it back to a solid. This completes the separation process.

Freeze-dried foods are usually more expensive initially but they have an amazing shelf life of up to 25-30 years unopened and 6-18 months once opened. These are a great way to add fruits and vegetables to your food storage that may otherwise be hard

---

[1] Shelf Reliance Staff, Sept 22nd 2009. See more at www.shelfreliance.com

to come by or bottle. Freeze dried foods actually have a higher nutritional value than food from your grocery store in most cases. This is because the food is allowed to ripen on the vine or tree before being freeze dried which allows the food to absorb more nutrients, then the freeze drying process locks them in. Unlike normal food which is picked before ripening so it doesn't spoil during the shipping process. Most "fresh" foods in the grocery store were picked 21+ days before arriving at the store.

I use freeze dried foods in my daily cooking. Not only is the flavor amazing, but it's convenient and we have less waste with the extended shelf life and ability to only use what we need per recipe.

There are different companies that offer freeze dried foods, however I highly recommend Thrive Life. I used their products for over 10 years before becoming a consultant. I can't vouch for the quality or ingredients of other companies, but I can say I am very impressed with Thrive Life and they don't add any artificial flavors, colorings, or fillers and there's no GMO's. If you'd like to try their products out order through my website and you can get wholesale pricing.

www.what8ate.thrivelife.com

Dehydrated foods

Dehydrating foods can be done with your own dehydrator. Beef jerky, banana chips, fruit leather, apple slices, and other foods can be dehydrated for a longer shelf life. It is recommended that once you dehydrate the food vacuum pack in either a bag or glass jar for extended freshness and quality.

Dehydrated foods can be eaten after adding water or as they are.

Fruit Leather can be made by simply pureeing the desired fruit, adding lemon juice to prevent color changing, sugar (if needed) and then spreading it onto waxed paper and placed in the dehydrator to process. Some people even add jell-o, or food coloring for added flavor and appearance. Be sure to spread it out thin before drying.

Water Storage

Water should also be stored as part of your food storage. Purchasing and filling some 55 gallon barrels of water is a good way to make sure your family will have the water they need. You can even get pumps for these barrels to make access easier. Remember you will need water for drinking, food preparation, washing clothes & bodies, and sanitizing. To reduce the amount of water needed for cleaning make sure you have baby wipes for washing hands and bodies, and Clorox or Lysol wipes for cleaning and sanitizing.

Water should be rotated every year to avoid bacteria build up. A bottle of water purifying drops is also handy in case of water contamination. Household bleach can be used to purify water or boiling the water. Purchase water litmus strips to test your water and check to make sure your water is in need of being purified before adding anything. A good rule of thumb for water storage is 1 gallon of water per person per day.
Be careful with bottled water, the plastic can leak chemicals into the water over time, especially if it's kept in a warm or hot environment. Water filters and pitchers are a great addition to have in your food storage!

Food Storage Check List

Using the included check list as an example or draft, list each consumable item your family uses. As you will see in my list that includes everything from food, batteries, toiletries, and supplies. Basically anything you would need if there were no more stores to purchase them from.

Once you have a list of all the consumable items your family uses list how much you use of each item per month, or how many months one item will last you. For example, you may use 24 rolls of toilet paper, and 6 cans of cream of chicken soup in one month, but one large tub of laundry soap will last you 2 months. So mark them accordingly in the Use/Monthly column as "6 cans" or "1 tub=2 months". It is always better to have too much than not enough so I ALWAYS overestimate how much we use in a month. We may use ¾ of a bottle of ketchup, but I will put 1 bottle. This will do 2 things: first you will in reality have a little more food storage than you think you do, and secondly, if in an emergency you need to feed more than just your family you will have enough.

Now that you have a list of all the items your family uses and how much they use per month you can easily figure out how many months' supply you have and need of each item. At one quick glance of your chart it is easy to figure out what items you need to buy more of and how much you need.

The good thing about doing food storage this way is you are purchasing food that you use on a regular basis. Who wants to go from pizza, fast food and all the good stuff we have now to living off wheat and beans? So put the things in your food storage that your family eats now.   If your family does eat a lot of fast food or store-bought premade food items it'd be a good idea to start making some homemade meals now for health as well as to get your family used to eating food and ingredients you can store. If you eat premade foods because of time restraints then making freezer meals would be a good way to transition from processed premade foods in the store, to good healthful homemade meals.

Here is the list; you can also get an **updated version** of it in digital format in our Food Storage 101 group on facebook at www.facebook.com/groups/foodstorage101 once you download it you can add/remove items and customize it for your family. The list below is an example; feel free to copy and use it, or use it as a reference to make your own. Here is an example of what your list might look like if you had 1 bottle of Advil and 8 boxes of brownie mix; checking the month's supply of each item according to how much your family uses per month.

Food Storage Item	amount/month	1	2	3	4	5	6	7	8	9	10	11	12
Advil	1 bottle= 3 months	X	X	X									
Brownie Mix	4 boxes= 1 month	X	X										

So as you can see from this example, you would have a 3-month supply of Advil, and a 2-month supply of brownie mix.

Food Storage Item	amount/month	1	2	3	4	5	6	7	8	9	10	11	12
Advil													
Air Fresheners--Carpet Powder													
Air Fresheners--room décor													
Allergy Medicine													
Applesauce													
Baking Powder													
Baking Soda													
Band-Aids													
Batteries-- AAA													
Batteries-- AA													
Batteries-- C													
Batteries-- D													
Batteries-- 9 Volt													
BBQ Sauce													
Bisquick													
Bleach													
Body Soap													
Bottled Water													
Bounce Fabric Sheets													

Brown Sugar													
Food Storage Item	**amount/month**	**1**	**2**	**3**	**4**	**5**	**6**	**7**	**8**	**9**	**10**	**11**	**12**
Brownie Mix													
Cereal													
Children's Allergy Medicine													
Children's Cold Medicine													
Children's Tylenol													
Chips													
Chocolate Chips													
Cinnamon													
Club Crackers													
Cocoa Powder													
Contact Solution													
Contacts													
Corn													
Cough Drops													
Cough Syrup													
Cranberry Sauce													
Cream of Chicken Soup													
Cream of Mushroom Soup													
Crisco													
Deodorant													
Desitin													
Diapers													
Dish Soap													
Dishwasher Soap													
Disinfectant/cleaner													
Drink Mix/Kool--Aid													
Evaporated Milk													
Extracts-- mint, root beer etc.													

Food Storage Item	amount/month	1	2	3	4	5	6	7	8	9	10	11	12
Fabric Softener													
Flashlight													
Flour													
Fruit cocktail													
Graham Crackers													
Green Beans													
Honey													
Hydrogen Peroxide													
Instant Potatoes													
Karo Syrup													
Ketchup													
Kleenex													
Laundry Soap													
Lemon Juice													
Mac & Cheese													
Make-up--foundation													
Make-up--mascara													
Make-up--eyeliner													
Make-up--lipstick													
Make-up--eyebrow liner													
Make-up--lip liner													
Make-up--blush													
Make-up-- eye shadow													
Mandarin Oranges													
Maple Extract													
Mayo													
Muffin Mix													
Mushrooms													
Mustard													
Noodles													

Nutmeg													
Food Storage Item	**amount/month**	**1**	**2**	**3**	**4**	**5**	**6**	**7**	**8**	**9**	**10**	**11**	**12**
Nyquil													
Oatmeal-- Instant													
Olive Oil													
Pads- feminine needs													
Paper													
Paper Plates													
Paper Towels													
Pens													
Pineapple-- crushed, cubed, rings													
Powdered Milk													
Powdered Sugar													
Q-tips													
Quick Oats													
Razors/blades													
Rice													
Ritz Crackers													
Rubbing Alcohol													
salad dressing													
Salt													
Sea Salt													
Seasonings													
Shampoo/Conditioner													
Soy Sauce													
Stewed Tomatoes													
Stuffing													
Sugar													
Sweetened Condensed Milk													
Swiffer Cleaner													

Swiffer Pads														
Food Storage Item	**amount/month**	**1**	**2**	**3**	**4**	**5**	**6**	**7**	**8**	**9**	**10**	**11**	**12**
Swiffer Vac Pads														
Tampons														
Toilet Paper														
Tomato Soup														
Tooth Brushes														
Tooth Paste														
Tylenol														
Vanilla														
Vaseline														
Vegetable Oil														
Water-- large container														
Wheat														
Wipes														
Worcestershire Sauce														
Yeast														

Freezer Foods														
Food Storage Item	**amount/month**	**1**	**2**	**3**	**4**	**5**	**6**	**7**	**8**	**9**	**10**	**11**	**12**
Broccoli														
Brussel Sprouts														
Butter														
Carrots														

Chicken Breasts													
Food Storage Item	**amount/month**	**1**	**2**	**3**	**4**	**5**	**6**	**7**	**8**	**9**	**10**	**11**	**12**
Chicken Tenders/Strips													
Ground Beef													
Ham													
Hamburger Patties													
Hash Browns													
Hotdogs													
Ice Cream													
Juice													
Mixed Veggies													
Peaches													
Popsicles													
Pork Chops													
Pork Ribs													
Roast													
Salsa Mix													
Sausage													
Shredded Cheese													
Steak													
Strawberries													
Turkey-- Whole													

Recommended Staples

These are items that I ALWAYS have in my house and food storage because they are the things that get used the most, the things we couldn't/wouldn't want to cook without or the items that are key to recipes. For the butter, I bottle or freeze it. For the milk and eggs I have the powdered forms or substitutes.

Baking powder	Garlic and herb	Powdered
Baking soda	seasoning	Sugar
BBQ sauce	Garlic Powder	Rice
Beef bouillon	Gelatin	Salad Seasoning
Bisquick	Graham	Salt
Bread Crumbs	Crackers	Seasoned Salt
Brown Sugar	Honey	Soy Sauce
Butter	Italian	Stuffing Mix
Canola Oil	Seasoning	Sugar
Chicken	Jell-o	Sweet &
Bouillon	Karo Syrup	Condensed Milk
Chocolate Chips	Ketchup	Unflavored
Cinnamon	Maple Flavoring	Gelatin
Cocoa Powder	Mayo	Vanilla Extract
Cornmeal	Minced Garlic	Vinegar
Cornstarch	Mustard	Wheat
Crisco	Nutmeg	Worchester
Dried Onions	Oatmeal	Sauce
Dried Parsley	Olive Oil	Yeast
Evaporated	Pancake Syrup	
Milk	Popcorn salt	
Flour	Popcorn seeds	
Fruit Jam	Powdered Milk	

A Complete Years Food Supply in One Year

The following list is one I received from Relief Society and would give credit to whoever compiled it if I knew who that was. This list would be for basic food storage. Perfect for those that do not do a lot of cooking, or like to keep things simple.

The idea with this list is to each week set aside $10 to purchase the food storage items for that week. Some weeks you may have extra left over, save the extra for those weeks when you may need more than $10.00. This list is enough to sustain two people for one year. For a larger family multiply as needed.

Week 1: 6 lbs. of salt
Week 2: 5 cans cream of
    chicken soup
Week 3: 20 # sugar
Week 4: 8 cans tomato soup
Week 5: 50 # wheat
Week 6: 6 # macaroni
Week 7: 20 lbs. sugar
Week 8: 8 cans tuna
Week 9: 6 lbs. yeast
Week 10: 50 lbs. wheat
Week 11: 8 cans tomato soup
Week 12: 20 # sugar
Week 13: 20 # powdered milk
Week 14: 7 boxes macaroni &
    cheese
Week 15: 50 # wheat
Week 16: 5 cans cream of
    chicken soup
Week 17:1 bottle of 500
    multi-vitamins
Week 18: 10 # powdered milk
Week 19: 5 cans cream
    mushroom soup
Week 20: 50 # wheat
Week 21: 8 cans tomato soup
Week 22: 20 # sugar
Week 23: 8 cans tuna
Week 24: 6 # shortening
Week 25: 50 # wheat
Week 26: 5 # honey
Week 27: 10 # powdered milk
Week 28: 20 # sugar
Week 29: 5 # peanut butter
Week 30: 50 #. wheat
Week 31: 7 boxes macaroni &

cheese
Week 32: 10 # powdered milk
Week 33: 1 bottle of 50 aspirin
Week 34: 5 cans cream of
    chicken soup
Week 35: 50 # wheat
Week 36: 7 boxes macaroni &
    cheese
Week 37: 6 # salt
Week 38: 20 # sugar
Week 39: 8 cans tomato soup
Week 40: 50 # wheat
Week 41: 5 cans cream of
chicken soup

Week 42: 20 #. sugar
Week 43: 1 bottle of 500
    multi-vitamins
Week 44: 8 cans tuna
Week 45: 50 # wheat
Week 46: 6 # macaroni
Week 47: 20 # sugar
Week 48: 5 cans cream
    mushroom soup
Week 49: 5 # honey
Week 50: 20 # sugar
Week 51: 8 cans tomato soup
Week 52: 50 # wheat

At the end of one year you will have:

500 lbs. wheat	45 cans tomato soup	15 cans cream mushroom
12 lbs. salt	500 Aspirin	15 cans cream of chicken
5 lbs. peanut butter	6 lbs. yeast	21 boxes macaroni & cheese
24 cans of tuna	12 lbs. macaroni	6 lbs. shortening
1,000 multi-vitamins	40 lbs. powdered milk	
180 lbs. sugar		
10 lbs. honey		

*totals will be different if you have multiplied for more family members.

52 Weeks of Little by Little

The Following is a week by week guide to small things you can do each week to achieve a goal by the end of the year. It is a challenge I had on my blog, and have added to the revised version of this book since it goes along with the same concept as Little by Little.

These weekly guides are a great way to accomplish a large goal, by doing simple and easy things each week.

You can do one, multiple, or all of them- it's up to you! Don't overwhelm yourself. And remember, if you start off with doing a lot of them then don't have time for all of them, that's okay! Just cut back to the ones that are most important to you and tackle others another year, or once a week, etc.

This is meant to be something to simplify and reduce stress- eating the elephant one bite at a time sort of speak. If it causes you more anxiety, you're putting too much pressure on yourself- stop thinking about the elephant and start thinking about the bites each week.

If you don't know that elephant reference- it's basically "how do you eat an elephant?" "one bite at a time" meaning that no one can do something grand all at once, so don't put those expectations on yourself, however, taking one bite (step) at a time you will reach your ultimate goal.

We also have a facebook group that offers support and encouragement with this guide, it's free. Search for "52 weeks of Little by Little" – we'd love to have you join us!

By the end of the year you will have accomplished:

- Clean & Organize
- Complete Projects on a To Do list
- Save $260-$1,040
- Try 52 New Recipes
- Work on Personal Development
- Improve Relationships
- Pay off debt
- Get healthy/lose weight
- BUILD A FOOD STORAGE

52 Weeks of Little By Little

Each week there will be a list of tasks to work on. By the end of the year you will have

- Clean & Organized
- Completed Projects on a To Do list
- Saved $260-$1040
- Get healthy/lose weight
- Tried 52 New Recipes
- Worked on Personal Development
- Improved Relationships
- BUILT A FOOD STORAGE
- Pay off debt

www.atozformomslikeme.blogspot.com

Week 1:

Kitchen counters & Sink
Make a list of projects
Set aside $5-20

Crockpot funeral potatoes
Make a list of personal goals
Call 3 people just to say "hi"
BUY 6LBS SALT

*If you always do
What you've always done,
You'll always get
What you've always got*

Make a list of all debt
Weigh & Measure yourself

* * * * * * * * * * * * * * * *

52 Weeks of Little By Little

Each week there will be a list of tasks to work on. By the end of the year you will have

- Clean & Organized
- Completed Projects on a To Do list
- Saved $260-$1040
- Get healthy/lose weight
- Tried 52 New Recipes
- Worked on Personal Development
- Improved Relationships
- BUILT A FOOD STORAGE
- Pay off debt

www.atozformomslikeme.blogspot.com

Week 2:

Kitchen cabinets & drawers
Fix 1 thing you've been putting off
Set aside $5-20

Chicken Gnocchi Soup
Read at least 4 chapters of a book
Write a letter and mail it
BUY 5 CANS OF CREAM OF CHICKEN SOUP

*Even if you're on the right
track, you'll get run over
if you sit there!*

List debt balances low/high
Drink lots of water! 100+oz

52 Weeks of Little By Little

Each week there will be a list of tasks to work on. By the end of the year you will have

- Clean & Organized
- Completed Projects on a To Do list
- Saved $260-$1040
- Get healthy/lose weight
- Tried 52 New Recipes
- Worked on Personal Development
- Improved Relationships
- BUILT A FOOD STORAGE
- Pay off debt

Week 3:

www.atozformomslikeme.blogspot.com

Pantry & food storage
Organizing project
Set aside $5-20

Meatloaf
Make a Life Vision Poster
Text 10 people to say "hi"
BUY 20LBS OF SUGAR

You only live once, but if you do it right once is enough.

Schedule your bills
Create a menu plan

*** * * * * * * * * * * * * * ***

52 Weeks of Little By Little

Each week there will be a list of tasks to work on. By the end of the year you will have

- Clean & Organized
- Completed Projects on a To Do list
- Saved $260-$1040
- Get healthy/lose weight
- Tried 52 New Recipes
- Worked on Personal Development
- Improved Relationships
- BUILT A FOOD STORAGE
- Pay off debt

Week 4:

www.atozformomslikeme.blogspot.com

Fridge & freezer
Project for the kitchen
Set aside $5-20

5 Decker Dinner
Read at least 4 chapters of a book
Introduce yourself to someone new
BUY 8 CANS OF TOMATO SOUP

Make today a better day than yesterday.

Apply soda $ to a bill
Walk around the block

52 Weeks of Little By Little

Each week there will be a list of tasks to work on. By the end of the year you will have

- Clean & Organized
- Completed Projects on a To Do list
- Saved $260-$1040
- Get healthy/lose weight

- Tried 52 New Recipes
- Worked on Personal Development
- Improved Relationships
- BUILT A FOOD STORAGE
- Pay off debt

www.atozformomslikeme.blogspot.com

Week 5:

Mail

Mail & Bill Organized system

Set aside $5-20

Shepherd's Pie

Write in your journal

Give a treat to a neighbor

BUY 10LBS OF FLOUR

By small & simple things are great things brought to pass.

Make $20 extra for a bill

Fix healthy snacks

****

52 Weeks of Little By Little

Each week there will be a list of tasks to work on. By the end of the year you will have

- Clean & Organized
- Completed Projects on a To Do list
- Saved $260-$1040
- Get healthy/lose weight

- Tried 52 New Recipes
- Worked on Personal Development
- Improved Relationships
- BUILT A FOOD STORAGE
- Pay off debt

www.atozformomslikeme.blogspot.com

Week 6:

Recipes & cook books

Pick a project for a window

Set aside $5-20

BBQ Drumsticks

Meditate for 30 minutes

Tell 5 people something you admire about them

BUY 6LBS MACARONI

It's better to prepare & prevent than to repair & repent.

Budgeting date night

Find ways to "move it, move it"

52 Weeks of *Little By Little*

Each week there will be a list of tasks to work on. By the end of the year you will have

- Clean & Organized
- Completed Projects on a To Do list
- Saved $260-$1040
- Get healthy/lose weight

- Tried 52 New Recipes
- Worked on Personal Development
- Improved Relationships
- BUILT A FOOD STORAGE
- Pay off debt

www.atozformomslikeme.blogspot.com

Week 7:

Receipts and Tax documents
Long term filing system
Set aside $5-20

Chicken & Broccoli Casserole
Read an article about someone you admire
Do 3 random acts of kindness
BUY 20LBS OF SUGAR

Your Attitude Determines your Altitude!

Make a double payment
Reduce your carb & sugars

****

52 Weeks of *Little By Little*

Each week there will be a list of tasks to work on. By the end of the year you will have

- Clean & Organized
- Completed Projects on a To Do list
- Saved $260-$1040
- Get healthy/lose weight

- Tried 52 New Recipes
- Worked on Personal Development
- Improved Relationships
- BUILT A FOOD STORAGE
- Pay off debt

www.atozformomslikeme.blogspot.com

Week 8:

Coupons & Purse
Pick a project for a decoration
Set aside $5-20

Biscuits and Sausage Gravy
Put affirmations on your mirror
Send a letter to a family member
BUY 8 CANS OF TUNA

Your outside reflect your inside.

Pay a little extra on one
Weigh & Measure yourself

52 Weeks of Little By Little

Each week there will be a list of tasks to work on. By the end of the year you will have

- Clean & Organized
- Completed Projects on a To Do list
- Saved $260-$1040
- Get healthy/lose weight
- Tried 52 New Recipes
- Worked on Personal Development
- Improved Relationships
- BUILT A FOOD STORAGE
- Pay off debt

www.atozformomslikeme.blogspot.com

Week 9:

Meal Planning & Grocery lists
Weekly meal chart
Set aside $5-20

Aussie Chicken
Pamper yourself
Write a list of 10 things you love about someone
BUY 6LBS OF YEAST

Happiness comes from within.

Sell something and pay extra
Do 10 lunges before dessert

* * * * * * * * * * * * * * * *

52 Weeks of Little By Little

Each week there will be a list of tasks to work on. By the end of the year you will have

- Clean & Organized
- Completed Projects on a To Do list
- Saved $260-$1040
- Get healthy/lose weight
- Tried 52 New Recipes
- Worked on Personal Development
- Improved Relationships
- BUILT A FOOD STORAGE
- Pay off debt

www.atozformomslikeme.blogspot.com

Week 10:

Living room
Fabric project
Set aside $5-20

Chili
Write 10 things you're grateful for
Hug 5 people for 10 seconds or more
BUY 10LBS OF FLOUR

Everything is Awesome!

Make a double payment
Add lemon to your water

52 Weeks of Little By Little

Each week there will be a list of tasks to work on. By the end of the year you will have

- Clean & Organized
- Completed Projects on a To Do list
- Saved $260-$1040
- Get healthy/lose weight
- Tried 52 New Recipes
- Worked on Personal Development
- Improved Relationships
- BUILT A FOOD STORAGE
- Pay off debt

Week 11:

www.atozformomslikeme.blogspot.com

Cleaning Supplies
Pantry Organizing Project
Set aside $5-20

Chicken Alfredo
Write down some year-long goals
Buy something for someone just because
BUY 8 CANS OF TOMATO SOUP

Dream it, Wish it, Do it!

Pay $10 extra
Try new green salad ideas

∗∗∗∗∗∗∗∗∗∗∗∗∗∗∗∗

52 Weeks of Little By Little

Each week there will be a list of tasks to work on. By the end of the year you will have

- Clean & Organized
- Completed Projects on a To Do list
- Saved $260-$1040
- Get healthy/lose weight
- Tried 52 New Recipes
- Worked on Personal Development
- Improved Relationships
- BUILT A FOOD STORAGE
- Pay off debt

Week 12:

www.atozformomslikeme.blogspot.com

Bathroom
Painting project
Set aside $5-20

Crockpot BBQ Beef Sandwiches
Read 4 chapters of a book
Get to know someone better
BUY 20LBS OF SUGAR

Whatever the mind can conceive, it can achieve.

Use fun money for a bill
Create a workout playlist

52 Weeks of Little By Little

Each week there will be a list of tasks to work on. By the end of the year you will have

- Clean & Organized
- Completed Projects on a To Do list
- **Saved $260-$1040**
- Get healthy/lose weight
- Tried 52 New Recipes
- Worked on Personal Development
- Improved Relationships
- **BUILT A FOOD STORAGE**
- Pay off debt

Week 13:

www.atozformomslikeme.blogspot.com

Windows
Organizing Project
Set aside $5-20

Winger's Copycat wings
Meditate for 15 minutes
Make a treat for someone
BUY 10 LBS POWDERED MILK

Happiness is what happiness does.

Pay $50 extra on a bill
Take a multivitimin

* * * * * * * * * * * * * * * * * *

52 Weeks of Little By Little

Each week there will be a list of tasks to work on. By the end of the year you will have

- Clean & Organized
- Completed Projects on a To Do list
- **Saved $260-$1040**
- Get healthy/lose weight
- Tried 52 New Recipes
- Worked on Personal Development
- Improved Relationships
- **BUILT A FOOD STORAGE**
- Pay off debt

Week 14:

www.atozformomslikeme.blogspot.com

Vacuum all edges
Outside Project
Set aside $5-20

Ham & Split Pea Soup
Manicure/Pedicure
Make eye contact
BUY 7 BOXES OF MAC & CHEESE

Smile! It's Contagious!

Update your debt list
Do yoga or stretching

52 Weeks of Little By Little

Each week there will be a list of tasks to work on. By the end of the year you will have

- Clean & Organized
- Completed Projects on a To Do list
- Saved $260-$1040
- Get healthy/lose weight
- Tried 52 New Recipes
- Worked on Personal Development
- Improved Relationships
- BUILT A FOOD STORAGE
- Pay off debt

Week 15:

www.atozformomslikeme.blogspot.com

Magazines & Newspapers
Rearrange Time!
Set aside $5-20

Hobo Dinners
Make a list
Call an old friend
BUY 10 LBS OF FLOUR

An ounce of prevention is worth a pound of cure.

Skip coffee/soda and pay it on a bill
Double your water intake

*** * * * * * * * * * * * * * * * ***

52 Weeks of Little By Little

Each week there will be a list of tasks to work on. By the end of the year you will have

- Clean & Organized
- Completed Projects on a To Do list
- Saved $260-$1040
- Get healthy/lose weight
- Tried 52 New Recipes
- Worked on Personal Development
- Improved Relationships
- BUILT A FOOD STORAGE
- Pay off debt

Week 16:

www.atozformomslikeme.blogspot.com

Trash Cans
Bathroom project
Set aside $5-20

Fruit Salsa
Read 4 chapters
Invite someone to lunch
BUY 5 CANS CR. OF CHICKEN SOUP

Just do it!

Eat cheap and put the extra $ towards a bill
Eat more fruits & veggies

52 Weeks of Little By Little

Each week there will be a list of tasks to work on. By the end of the year you will have

- Clean & Organized
- Completed Projects on a To Do list
- Saved $260-$1040
- Get healthy/lose weight
- Tried 52 New Recipes
- Worked on Personal Development
- Improved Relationships
- BUILT A FOOD STORAGE
- Pay off debt

www.atozformomslikeme.blogspot.com

Week 17:

Filing System
Dining Room Project
Set aside $5-20

Lazy BBQ Chicken
Evaluate goals list
Touch when talking to someone
BUY 500 MULTIVITAMINS

Stop wishing, start doing!

Use gift $, make homemade
Skip or run as much as possible

*** * * * * * * * * * * * * * * ***

52 Weeks of Little By Little

Each week there will be a list of tasks to work on. By the end of the year you will have

- Clean & Organized
- Completed Projects on a To Do list
- Saved $260-$1040
- Get healthy/lose weight
- Tried 52 New Recipes
- Worked on Personal Development
- Improved Relationships
- BUILT A FOOD STORAGE
- Pay off debt

www.atozformomslikeme.blogspot.com

Week 18:

Bathroom
Bathroom project
Set aside $5-20

Steak Blankets
Read 4 chapters
Learn something new about someone
BUY 10 LBS POWDERED MILK

Mistakes are proof that you're trying!

Earn $20 extra for a bill
Eat 6 small meals

52 Weeks of Little By Little

Each week there will be a list of tasks to work on. By the end of the year you will have

- Clean & Organized
- Completed Projects on a To Do list
- Saved $260-$1040
- Get healthy/lose weight
- Tried 52 New Recipes
- Worked on Personal Development
- Improved Relationships
- BUILT A FOOD STORAGE
- Pay off debt

Week 19:

www.atozformomslikeme.blogspot.com

Medicines
Deep clean project
Set aside $5-20

New York Cheesecake
Meditate for 30 minutes
Invite someone over for dinner
BUY 5 CANS CR. OF MUSHROOM SOUP

You don't have to be great to start, but you have to start to be great!

Find unnecessary expenses
Eat healthy fats

✳✳✳✳✳✳✳✳✳✳✳✳✳✳✳✳

52 Weeks of Little By Little

Each week there will be a list of tasks to work on. By the end of the year you will have

- Clean & Organized
- Completed Projects on a To Do list
- Saved $260-$1040
- Get healthy/lose weight
- Tried 52 New Recipes
- Worked on Personal Development
- Improved Relationships
- BUILT A FOOD STORAGE
- Pay off debt

Week 20:

www.atozformomslikeme.blogspot.com

Entry way
Front door project
Set aside $5-20

Parmesan Tilapia
Stretch for 30 minutes
Thank you gift
BUY 10 LBS OF FLOUR

The best way to predict the future is to create it

Eliminate 1 expense from last weeks list- pay bill
RUN around the block

52 Weeks of Little By Little

Each week there will be a list of tasks to work on. By the end of the year you will have

- Clean & Organized
- Completed Projects on a To Do list
- Saved $260-$1040
- Get healthy/lose weight
- Tried 52 New Recipes
- Worked on Personal Development
- Improved Relationships
- BUILT A FOOD STORAGE
- Pay off debt

www.atozformomslikeme.blogspot.com

Week 21:

Living Room
Couches
Set aside $5-20

Veggie Lasagna

Dream

Call 5 people just to say "hi"

BUY 8 CANS TOMATO SOUP

It's hard to beat a person that never gives up- Babe Ruth

Pay $25 extra on a bill

Listen to your body

****

52 Weeks of Little By Little

Each week there will be a list of tasks to work on. By the end of the year you will have

- Clean & Organized
- Completed Projects on a To Do list
- Saved $260-$1040
- Get healthy/lose weight
- Tried 52 New Recipes
- Worked on Personal Development
- Improved Relationships
- BUILT A FOOD STORAGE
- Pay off debt

www.atozformomslikeme.blogspot.com

Week 22:

Family Room
Entertainment
Set aside $5-20

Strawberry Cheesecake Dip

Make a To Do list

Invite someone on a picnic

BUY 20 LBS OF SUGAR

Work, until your idols become your rivals.

Use cash only

Cut back on carbs

52 Weeks of Little By Little

Each week there will be a list of tasks to work on. By the end of the year you will have

- Clean & Organized
- Completed Projects on a To Do list
- Saved $260-$1040
- Get healthy/lose weight
- Tried 52 New Recipes
- Worked on Personal Development
- Improved Relationships
- BUILT A FOOD STORAGE
- Pay off debt

Week 23:

www.atozformomslikeme.blogspot.com

Dining Room
Entertaining
Set aside $5-20

Crockpot Mashed Potatoes
Read 4 chapters
Do an act of secret service
BUY 8 CANS OF TUNA

Work hard, Dream big!

Make a double payment
Weigh & Measure yourself

* * * * * * * * * * * * * * * *

52 Weeks of Little By Little

Each week there will be a list of tasks to work on. By the end of the year you will have

- Clean & Organized
- Completed Projects on a To Do list
- Saved $260-$1040
- Get healthy/lose weight
- Tried 52 New Recipes
- Worked on Personal Development
- Improved Relationships
- BUILT A FOOD STORAGE
- Pay off debt

Week 24:

www.atozformomslikeme.blogspot.com

Laundry Room
Landry room project
Set aside $5-20

Chicken Enchilada Dip
Meditate for 30 minutes
Host a game night
BUY 6LBS SHORTENING

You are the only you there is!

Create a debt-free dream
YouTube workout

52 Weeks of Little By Little

Each week there will be a list of tasks to work on. By the end of the year you will have

- Clean & Organized
- Completed Projects on a To Do list
- **Saved $260–$1040**
- Get healthy/lose weight
- Tried 52 New Recipes
- Worked on Personal Development
- **Improved Relationships**
- **BUILT A FOOD STORAGE**
- Pay off debt

Week 25:
www.atozformomslikeme.blogspot.com

Dirty & Clean clothes areas
Laundry basket project
Set aside $5-20

Pomegranate Raspberry Salad
Stretch for 30 minutes
Compliment 10 people
BUY 10 LBS FLOUR

Today is the tomorrow you worried about yesterday.

Lunch money for bills
Fruit is dessert

* * * * * * * * * * * * * * * * * *

52 Weeks of Little By Little

Each week there will be a list of tasks to work on. By the end of the year you will have

- Clean & Organized
- Completed Projects on a To Do list
- **Saved $260–$1040**
- Get healthy/lose weight
- Tried 52 New Recipes
- Worked on Personal Development
- **Improved Relationships**
- **BUILT A FOOD STORAGE**
- Pay off debt

Week 26:
www.atozformomslikeme.blogspot.com

Purse/wallet
Money project
Set aside $5-20

Strawberry Coconut Amaretto
Reflect on your progress
Host a dinner/bbq
BUY 5LBS HONEY

Half full, or half empty– either way you have room for more!

Pay $25 extra on a bill
Double your water intake

52 Weeks of *Little By Little*

Each week there will be a list of tasks to work on. By the end of the year you will have

- Clean & Organized
- Completed Projects on a To Do list
- Saved $260-$1040
- Get healthy/lose weight
- Tried 52 New Recipes
- Worked on Personal Development
- Improved Relationships
- BUILT A FOOD STORAGE
- Pay off debt

Week 27:

www.atozformomslikeme.blogspot.com

Bookcase

Shelf, bookcase, storage project

Set aside $5-20

Samoa Brownies

Write in your journal

Call your family

BUY 10 LBS POWDERED MILK

Always be yourself, unless you can be batman, then always be batman.

Update debt list

Squats & lunges all day

****

52 Weeks of *Little By Little*

Each week there will be a list of tasks to work on. By the end of the year you will have

- Clean & Organized
- Completed Projects on a To Do list
- Saved $260-$1040
- Get healthy/lose weight
- Tried 52 New Recipes
- Worked on Personal Development
- Improved Relationships
- BUILT A FOOD STORAGE
- Pay off debt

Week 28:

www.atozformomslikeme.blogspot.com

Movies

Entertainment Center Project

Set aside $5-20

Disneyland Carmel Popcorn

Movie Night

Invite friends over for movie night

BUY 20 LBS SUGAR

They print more money every day- there's plenty!

Earn $20 extra for a bill

Find carb clones

52 Weeks of Little By Little

Each week there will be a list of tasks to work on. By the end of the year you will have

- Clean & Organized
- Completed Projects on a To Do list
- Saved $260-$1040
- Get healthy/lose weight

- Tried 52 New Recipes
- Worked on Personal Development
- Improved Relationships
- BUILT A FOOD STORAGE
- Pay off debt

www.atozformomslikeme.blogspot.com

Week 29:

Pictures on the wall
Family Pictures
Set aside $5-20

Mom's Trifle
Write family memories
Family night
BUY 5 LBS PEANUT BUTTER

Friend has a "end" but Family has "ILY= I love you"

Free date night- $ for bill
Dance any time you wait

* * * * * * * * * * * * * * * * * *

52 Weeks of Little By Little

Each week there will be a list of tasks to work on. By the end of the year you will have

- Clean & Organized
- Completed Projects on a To Do list
- Saved $260-$1040
- Get healthy/lose weight

- Tried 52 New Recipes
- Worked on Personal Development
- Improved Relationships
- BUILT A FOOD STORAGE
- Pay off debt

www.atozformomslikeme.blogspot.com

Week 30:

Craft Area
Craft Room Organization
Set aside $5-20

Stuffed Steak
30 minutes of stretching
30 second hug
BUY 10 LBS OF FLOUR

Hug others with real intent.

Homemade lunch/dinner
Find 10 healthy recipes

52 Weeks of Little By Little

Each week there will be a list of tasks to work on. By the end of the year you will have

- Clean & Organized
- Completed Projects on a To Do list
- Saved $260-$1040
- Get healthy/lose weight

- Tried 52 New Recipes
- Worked on Personal Development
- Improved Relationships
- BUILT A FOOD STORAGE
- Pay off debt

Week 31:

www.atozformomslikeme.blogspot.com

Cars
Travel project
Set aside $5-20

One Pan Breakfast
Goals Evaluation
Teacher gifts
BUY 7 BOXES OF MAC & CHEESE

If you can read this, thank a teacher!

Keep credit cards at home
Make an all veggie meal

****

52 Weeks of Little By Little

Each week there will be a list of tasks to work on. By the end of the year you will have

- Clean & Organized
- Completed Projects on a To Do list
- Saved $260-$1040
- Get healthy/lose weight

- Tried 52 New Recipes
- Worked on Personal Development
- Improved Relationships
- BUILT A FOOD STORAGE
- Pay off debt

Week 32:

www.atozformomslikeme.blogspot.com

Pet & related
Pet project
Set aside $5-20

Crock Pot Freezer Meals
Write in your journal
Send a thank you note
BUY 10 LBS OF POWDERED MILK

Always desire to learn something useful.

Walk instead of drive when possible
Drink your weight in oz of water

52 Weeks of Little By Little

Each week there will be a list of tasks to work on. By the end of the year you will have

- Clean & Organized
- Completed Projects on a To Do list
- Saved $260-$1090
- Get healthy/lose weight
- Tried 52 New Recipes
- Worked on Personal Development
- Improved Relationships
- BUILT A FOOD STORAGE
- Pay off debt

www.atozformomslikeme.blogspot.com

Week 33:

Garden
Garden Project
Set aside $5-20

Crock Pot Stroganoff
Learn something new
Give a friend a gift "just because"
BUY 1 BOTTLE OF 500 ASPRIN

Be happy. Be bright. Be you!

Replace $ with coupons
No elevator! Take the stairs!

✳✳✳✳✳✳✳✳✳✳✳✳✳✳✳✳

52 Weeks of Little By Little

Each week there will be a list of tasks to work on. By the end of the year you will have

- Clean & Organized
- Completed Projects on a To Do list
- Saved $260-$1090
- Get healthy/lose weight
- Tried 52 New Recipes
- Worked on Personal Development
- Improved Relationships
- BUILT A FOOD STORAGE
- Pay off debt

www.atozformomslikeme.blogspot.com

Week 34:

Yard
Landscaping Project
Set aside $5-20

Dutch Oven Potatoes
Go on a Nature walk
Send a card to 3 people
BUY 5 CANS CREAM OF CHICKEN SOUP

Be happy. Be bright. Be you!

Pay $20 extra on a bill
Jumping Jacks/trampoline

52 Weeks of Little By Little

Each week there will be a list of tasks to work on. By the end of the year you will have

- Clean & Organized
- Completed Projects on a To Do list
- Saved $260-$1040
- Get healthy/lose weight
- Tried 52 New Recipes
- Worked on Personal Development
- Improved Relationships
- BUILT A FOOD STORAGE
- Pay off debt

www.atozformomslikeme.blogspot.com

Week 35:

Tools & Shed
Organizing Project
Set aside $5-20

Enchilada's with White Sauce
Work on a specific goal
Check up on someone
BUY 10 LBS OF FLOUR

Always remember it has to be dark for stars to be seen.

Earn an extra $50
Say Positive affirmations

* * * * * * * * * * * * * * * *

52 Weeks of Little By Little

Each week there will be a list of tasks to work on. By the end of the year you will have

- Clean & Organized
- Completed Projects on a To Do list
- Saved $260-$1040
- Get healthy/lose weight
- Tried 52 New Recipes
- Worked on Personal Development
- Improved Relationships
- BUILT A FOOD STORAGE
- Pay off debt

www.atozformomslikeme.blogspot.com

Week 36:

Basement
DVD/Games organization project
Set aside $5-20

Fruit Pizza
Positive Affirmations
Give 10 good hugs
BUY 7 BOXES OF MAC & CHEESE

Life is not happening to you, life is responding to you.

Cancel 1 luxury
Find a healthy dessert recipe

52 Weeks of Little By Little

Each week there will be a list of tasks to work on. By the end of the year you will have

- Clean & Organized
- Completed Projects on a To Do list
- Saved $260-$1040
- Get healthy/lose weight
- Tried 52 New Recipes
- Worked on Personal Development
- Improved Relationships
- BUILT A FOOD STORAGE
- Pay off debt

www.atozformomslikeme.blogspot.com

Week 37:

Desks/Homework area
Office desk project
Set aside $5-20

Italian Chicken Bread
Stretch & Deep Breathing
Open doors for strangers
BUY 6 LBS OF SALT

Whatever you choose to do, make sure it makes you happy!

Balance your budget
Lift weights

****

52 Weeks of Little By Little

Each week there will be a list of tasks to work on. By the end of the year you will have

- Clean & Organized
- Completed Projects on a To Do list
- Saved $260-$1040
- Get healthy/lose weight
- Tried 52 New Recipes
- Worked on Personal Development
- Improved Relationships
- BUILT A FOOD STORAGE
- Pay off debt

www.atozformomslikeme.blogspot.com

Week 38:

Message area/keys/purse/mail
Landing Pad Creation
Set aside $5-20

Mini Sloppy Joe's
Bubble Bath
Smile at strangers
BUY 20 LBS OF SUGAR

Our thoughts determine our reality

Work 10 extra hours
Take a hot bath

52 Weeks of Little By Little

Each week there will be a list of tasks to work on. By the end of the year you will have

- Clean & Organized
- Completed Projects on a To Do list
- Saved $260~$1040
- Get healthy/lose weight

- Tried 52 New Recipes
- Worked on Personal Development
- Improved Relationships
- BUILT A FOOD STORAGE
- Pay off debt

www.atozformomslikeme.blogspot.com

Week 39:

Linen Closet
Towels/Sheets project
Set aside $5-20

Navajo Tacos
Dance to your favorite music!
Introduce 2 friends to each other
BUY 8 CANS OF TOMATO SOUP

Take a chance and don't ever look back!

Update your debt list
Run around the block

* * * * * * * * * * * * * * * * *

52 Weeks of Little By Little

Each week there will be a list of tasks to work on. By the end of the year you will have

- Clean & Organized
- Completed Projects on a To Do list
- Saved $260~$1040
- Get healthy/lose weight

- Tried 52 New Recipes
- Worked on Personal Development
- Improved Relationships
- BUILT A FOOD STORAGE
- Pay off debt

www.atozformomslikeme.blogspot.com

Week 40:

Hall closet
Closet Organization project
Set aside $5-20

Parmesan Chicken
Plan a trip
Text 10 people to say Hi
BUY 10 LBS OF FLOUR

Success doesn't come to you, you go to it!

Pay $100 extra on a bill
Do a cleanse

52 Weeks of Little By Little

Each week there will be a list of tasks to work on. By the end of the year you will have

- Clean & Organized
- Completed Projects on a To Do list
- Saved $260-$1040
- Get healthy/lose weight
- Tried 52 New Recipes
- Worked on Personal Development
- Improved Relationships
- BUILT A FOOD STORAGE
- Pay off debt

Week 41:

www.atozformomslikeme.blogspot.com

Bedroom Closets

Closet Shelves Project

Set aside $5-20

Pumpkin Chocolate Chip Cookies

Update your life vision board

Invite a friend to lunch

BUY 5 CANS CREAM OF CHICKEN SOUP

You are never too old to set another goal, or dream another dream. – C.S. Lewis

3 for 1 meal- make enough to last 3 meals

Have healthy snacks in the house

* * * * * * * * * * * * * * * *

52 Weeks of Little By Little

Each week there will be a list of tasks to work on. By the end of the year you will have

- Clean & Organized
- Completed Projects on a To Do list
- Saved $260-$1040
- Get healthy/lose weight
- Tried 52 New Recipes
- Worked on Personal Development
- Improved Relationships
- BUILT A FOOD STORAGE
- Pay off debt

Week 42:

www.atozformomslikeme.blogspot.com

Seasonal & Outgrown Clothing

Clothes Rotating system project

Set aside $5-20

Ranch Fried Chicken

Read 4 Chapters

Learn something new about a friend

BUY 20 LBS OF SUGAR

Life is short, smile while you still have teeth!

Game date night

Try a new sport

52 Weeks of Little By Little

Each week there will be a list of tasks to work on. By the end of the year you will have

- Clean & Organized
- Completed Projects on a To Do list
- Saved $260-$1040
- Get healthy/lose weight
- Tried 52 New Recipes
- Worked on Personal Development
- Improved Relationships
- BUILT A FOOD STORAGE
- Pay off debt

www.atozformomslikeme.blogspot.com

Week 43:

Master Bedroom
Master Bedroom Decoration
Set aside $5-20

Homemade Rice-a-roni
Meditate for 30 minutes
Give small treats to coworkers/teachers
BUY 1 BOTTLE OF 500 MULTIVITAMINS

All limitations are self imposed.

Make a double payment!
Eat a salad for lunch

✱✱✱✱✱✱✱✱✱✱✱✱✱✱✱✱

52 Weeks of Little By Little

Each week there will be a list of tasks to work on. By the end of the year you will have

- Clean & Organized
- Completed Projects on a To Do list
- Saved $260-$1040
- Get healthy/lose weight
- Tried 52 New Recipes
- Worked on Personal Development
- Improved Relationships
- BUILT A FOOD STORAGE
- Pay off debt

www.atozformomslikeme.blogspot.com

Week 44:

Garage
Garage Organization Project
Set aside $5-20

Sex in a Pan (5 layer dessert)
Buy a new outfit
Go to lunch with a friend
BUY 8 CANS OF TUNA

It's not happy people who are thankful, but thankful people who are happy.

Sell something and pay extra on a bill with the $
Pushups & sit-ups

52 Weeks of Little By Little

Each week there will be a list of tasks to work on. By the end of the year you will have

- Clean & Organized
- Completed Projects on a To Do list
- Saved $260-$1040
- Get healthy/lose weight

- Tried 52 New Recipes
- Worked on Personal Development
- Improved Relationships
- BUILT A FOOD STORAGE
- Pay off debt

Week 45:

www.atozformomslikeme.blogspot.com

Attic
Pick a project!
Set aside $5-20

Sweet & Sour Chicken
Quality "Me" time
Introduce yourself to someone new
BUY 10 LBS OF FLOUR

Believe in yourself and you can do unbelievable things!

Home vacation
Learn a cultural dance

✻ ✻ ✻ ✻ ✻ ✻ ✻ ✻ ✻ ✻ ✻ ✻ ✻ ✻

52 Weeks of Little By Little

Each week there will be a list of tasks to work on. By the end of the year you will have

- Clean & Organized
- Completed Projects on a To Do list
- Saved $260-$1040
- Get healthy/lose weight

- Tried 52 New Recipes
- Worked on Personal Development
- Improved Relationships
- BUILT A FOOD STORAGE
- Pay off debt

Week 46:

www.atozformomslikeme.blogspot.com

Jewelry & Accessories
Jewelry box/display project
Set aside $5-20

Sweet Potato Casserole
Read 4 chapters
Smile & wave to 20 random people
BUY 6 LBS OF PASTA

Quality means doing it right when no one is looking.

Pay $25 extra on a bill
Go for a nature walk

52 Weeks of Little By Little

Each week there will be a list of tasks to work on. By the end of the year you will have

- Clean & Organized
- Completed Projects on a To Do list
- Saved $260-$1040
- Get healthy/lose weight
- Tried 52 New Recipes
- Worked on Personal Development
- Improved Relationships
- BUILT A FOOD STORAGE
- Pay off debt

Week 47:

www.atozformomslikeme.blogspot.com

Shoes
Shoe project
Set aside $5-20

Homemade Turkey Soup
Gratitude List
Call 5 friends to say Hi
BUY 20 LBS OF SUGAR

Every minute is a chance to change.

Make it due instead of buying new
Drink lemon water instead of soda or coffee

★★★★★★★★★★★★★★★★★

52 Weeks of Little By Little

Each week there will be a list of tasks to work on. By the end of the year you will have

- Clean & Organized
- Completed Projects on a To Do list
- Saved $260-$1040
- Get healthy/lose weight
- Tried 52 New Recipes
- Worked on Personal Development
- Improved Relationships
- BUILT A FOOD STORAGE
- Pay off debt

Week 48:

www.atozformomslikeme.blogspot.com

Make-up & Cosmetics
Bathroom project
Set aside $5-20

Taco Salad
Read 4 Chapters
Text a silly picture to a friend
BUY 5 CANS CREAM OF MUSHROOM

If you can dream it, you can do it. —Walt Disney

Free date night- $ for bill
Do squats instead of standing

52 Weeks of Little By Little

Each week there will be a list of tasks to work on. By the end of the year you will have

- Clean & Organized
- Completed Projects on a To Do list
- Saved $260-$1040
- Get healthy/lose weight
- Tried 52 New Recipes
- Worked on Personal Development
- Improved Relationships
- BUILT A FOOD STORAGE
- Pay off debt

www.atozformomslikeme.blogspot.com

Week 49:

Kids' bedrooms
Kid bedroom project
Set aside $5-20

Sweet & Sour Pork Chops
List ways to serve others
Make dinner for someone
BUY 5 LBS OF HONEY

Most of us spend too much time on what is urgent and not enough time on what's important. —Steven Covey

Work 5 hours of overtime
Play a game of tag

*** * * * * * * * * * * * * * * * ***

52 Weeks of Little By Little

Each week there will be a list of tasks to work on. By the end of the year you will have

- Clean & Organized
- Completed Projects on a To Do list
- Saved $260-$1040
- Get healthy/lose weight
- Tried 52 New Recipes
- Worked on Personal Development
- Improved Relationships
- BUILT A FOOD STORAGE
- Pay off debt

www.atozformomslikeme.blogspot.com

Week 50:

Fancy/Serving Dishes
Party Project
Set aside $5-20

Pumpkin Rolls
Stretch for 30 minutes
Take a gift to neighbors
BUY 20 LBS OF SUGAR

Happiness is accepting life for what it is instead of what you want it to be.

Pay $25 extra on a bill
Reduce carbs and sugars

52 Weeks of Little By Little

Each week there will be a list of tasks to work on. By the end of the year you will have

- Clean & Organized
- Completed Projects on a To Do list
- Saved $260-$1090
- Get healthy/lose weight
- Tried 52 New Recipes
- Worked on Personal Development
- Improved Relationships
- BUILT A FOOD STORAGE
- Pay off debt

www.atozformomslikeme.blogspot.com

Week 51:

Holiday Decorations
Pick a holiday project!
Set aside $5-20

Tater Tot Casserole
Take a trip down Memory Lane
Call family members
BUY 8 CANS TOMATO SOUP

Do or do not, there is no try.
-Yoda

Pack a home lunch
Don't clear your plate

****

52 Weeks of Little By Little

Each week there will be a list of tasks to work on. By the end of the year you will have

- Clean & Organized
- Completed Projects on a To Do list
- Saved $260-$1090
- Get healthy/lose weight
- Tried 52 New Recipes
- Worked on Personal Development
- Improved Relationships
- BUILT A FOOD STORAGE
- Pay off debt

www.atozformomslikeme.blogspot.com

Week 52:

Family Calendar
Pick a project!
Set aside $5-20

Stuffed Mushrooms
Self Evaluation
Invite friends over for a Party!
BUY 10 LBS OF FLOUR

Today is a gift, that's why it's
called the present.

Review your debt list
Weigh & Measure yourself

Freezer Meal Recipes

These are recipes that you can make now and freeze in freezer/oven-safe containers to bake at a later time providing an easy dinner as a healthier and cheaper alternative to eating out.

5-Decker Dinner

This is an easy one-pan dish. If you want to throw something together and not worry about it while it cooks for 45 mins or so, and includes a good assortment from the food pyramid this is the recipe for you! My mom named it 5 Decker Dinner when she'd make it for us as kids. It can be layered uncooked into a freezer/oven container for a quick meal on another day too.

in a deep frying pan (or your freezer/oven container) layer:

(DO NOT turn on the burner yet though)

bacon

ground beef

sliced potatoes

(you can season the meat & potatoes if you desire)

then any assortment of veggies you like, I usually do carrots & broccoli

Cover with a lid, then turn the burner on LOW. You want this to cook slowly so the bacon doesn't burn.

After the potatoes are easily cut with a fork, sprinkle cheese on top and cook a couple more minutes until it's melted.

Best Meatloaf Ever!

I stumbled across this idea how to make meatloaf from watching a Rachel Ray show years ago and tweaked it a little. It makes the BEST meatloaf you will ever have! Even those who are not fans of meatloaf love this.

It's also another meal I make extra of for my freezer.

1-2 lbs of ground beef (depending on the size of your family)

1 box stove top stuffing mix (I use chicken-flavored, but you can do whatever kind you like)

2 eggs

1/2 c. ketchup

Mix well with your hands. You want to make sure you mix it enough so that the eggs, ketchup and stuffing are all through the meat- but DO NOT over-mix or your meat will be tough.

Place into a bread pan, form into a loaf-- and put in a casserole dish, or for a quicker meal put into a cupcake pan-- and create individual meatloaves for each person. Drizzle ketchup on top of the meat.

If making one big loaf- cover with tin foil and bake at 350 for 1 hour, remove tinfoil and bake for another 30 mins.
If making individual meatloaves in a cupcake pan- no covering is necessary. Bake at 350 for 45 mins.

This goes REALLY well with mashed sweet potatoes and peas.

For my freezer meals I used 1 5lb package of ground beef, 4 c. stuffing mix, 8 eggs, and about 1 c. ketchup-- this made 1 large bread pan size for tonight, and 3 small freezer pans

Chicken Broccoli Casserole

Ok this is a GREAT casserole! it's way yummy!
Before I list the recipe you'll see in the pictures 2 casseroles.
Every time I make a casserole, lasagna or something that takes a lot of time I make 2-5 times as much as we'll eat that night, and as I'm assembling it I put the extra into a freezable and bakeable dish. Smart N Final sells them with the lids that are silver on one

side and white on the other; they are perfect for the freezer then straight to the oven. This way I always have a home-cooked meal in the freezer. So these pictures represent a triple batch. Now for the recipe...

Boil chicken until cooked

Boil Broccoli until mostly cooked

Both of these can be as little or as much as your family likes. My family likes more veggies than meat so that's what I do.

Layer the chicken and broccoli in the pan evenly

In a bowl mix:

1-10 1/2 oz. cream of chicken soup
1/2 C milk
1 t lemon juice
3/4 C mayonnaise
1 C grated cheddar cheese
Then pour over chicken & broccoli
Sprinkle dry Stove-Top stuffing mix on top (approx 2 cups for 1 batch)
Melt 4 T butter and drizzle on top of stuffing

Bake at 350 for 40 mins, or until bubbly

Chicken Pot Pie

This is one of our favorites, it's really easy and you don't have to make a pie crust! It does take a long time to bake in order for the crust to cook fully though. But it's a great recipe to make with leftover veggies.

In a bowl combine:

1-2 cans cream of chicken soup

any mixture of your favorite veggies canned or frozen

chicken-- boiled & cut into chunks

Pour into a casserole dish or freezer/oven container.

In another bowl mix:

1-2 c. Bisquick

enough milk to make the mixture thin-- like pancake batter

Pour batter over chicken & veggies.

Cover with tinfoil. Bake at 325 for an hour, then remove tinfoil and bake until the center is done.

Enchiladas with White Sauce

Recently I heard these are also called Mormon Enchiladas... My grandma used to make them with corn tortillas; I prefer to use flour. These freeze easily.

Sauce:

1 can cream of chicken soup

1 can cream of mushroom soup

1 cup sour cream

1/2 small can of diced green chilies

cook 1lb ground beef with a little dried onions and Worcestershire.

Spread a little sauce in the bottom of the pan to prevent sticking. Spoon beef, a little chopped green onions (optional), a little of cheese, and 1-2 tablespoons of sauce in each tortilla, then roll up. Repeat until the pan is filled with completed enchiladas.

Bake at 350 for 20 minutes

Funeral Potatoes

Okay so first of all, this recipe is enough for one large 9x13 casserole, plus 3 small 6x8 freezer containers. As with any casserole it's just as easy to make a double or triple batch while you're doing it. So that's what I do and freeze the extra for quick and easy dinners in the future.

1 1/2 bunches of green onions, chopped

7 thick slices of ham, cubed

16 oz tub sour cream

3 cans cream of chicken soup

1 large bag of potato cubes (or shredded)

cheese, for topping

Mix first 4, then add potatoes, pour into casserole dish, then top with cheese. Bake at 350 for 30 minutes.

Lasagna

My husband's favorite food is lasagna so we have it at our house pretty often. It's pretty easy-- however makes a mess with a lot of dishes, so I always make extra to freeze for quick and mess less meals on other days. When I make this much I buy one bulk package of ground beef about 5lbs for the sauce. So adjust according to how much you're going to make!
This is a pretty easy process where you have multiple things going at once. Start the noodles, and while the meat is browning you can make the cheese mixture.

Cook lasagna noodles then let sit in cold water

Sauce:

cook ground beef

once beef is browned, add spaghetti sauce (either from a jar, or create your own with a mixture of pureed tomatoes, tomato sauce, tomato paste and Italian seasoning); I usually do some combination of the two.

Cheese:

2 large containers (32oz) cottage cheese

1 container (16 oz) Parmesan cheese (it really makes a difference to use the shredded rather than fine powder kind)

1/2- 1 c. spinach chopped (I add this for the extra vitamins my kids won't know about)

3-4 eggs

3 t. Italian seasoning

1-2 T. parsley (chopped or dried flakes)

Mix together well

In your pan(s) place a little of the sauce on the bottom to keep your noodles from sticking. Layer noodles across the bottom. Pour the cheese mixture on top of the noodles and spread out. Layer with more noodles on top of the cheese mixture. Pour the sauce on top. Then top with Mozzarella cheese.

Bake at 350 for 30 mins or until cheese is melted well.

Veggie Lasagna

This is the most amazing veggie lasagna you will ever taste! It's a great vegetarian meal, or just nice for something different like we did.

I improvised on a couple recipes I found online and this is what I came up with:

Alfredo sauce: (same as for my Alfredo chicken)

1 cube butter

8 oz cream cheese

melt together and whisk until well blended then add:

2 c. milk

1 t. garlic powder

1 tub of Parmesan cheese (16 oz)

Cook until desired thickness (will thicken a little as it cools)

Cottage cheese mixture:

1 tub cottage-cheese

1 bunch of fresh spinach, chopped

1-2 eggs

mix well.

In you pan spread a little of the sauce, then a layer of noodles. Spread the cottage-cheese mixture over the noodles, then layer with noodles again.

Sprinkle with shredded carrots and sliced mushrooms.

Spoon sauce over the top until the entire lasagna is well covered.

Sprinkle mozzarella cheese on top.

Bake at 350 for 25 minutes.

The first time I made this it was pretty watery; I precooked the noodles, so next time I am going to try making it with uncooked noodles.

Food Storage Recipes

We've all heard the stories about having to live off beans, rice and wheat if we ever needed to live off our food storage. Here are some recipes you can make with shelf-stable, bottled or other food-storage ingredients. Use the tips and techniques in this book to store some of the ingredients for longest shelf life and best flavor. And if you find a recipe you want to make just make sure you have all the ingredients in your food storage!

Apple Crisp

Food Storage Items:

- 1 can apple pie filling
- ½ box white cake mix[1]
- ½ cube butter[2]

Place pie filling in baking dish, sprinkle dry cake mix over top of pie filling, slice butter on top. Bake at 350 until golden brown.

BBQ Baked Beans

Food Storage Items:

---

[1] See instructions on how to store mixes in "vacuum packing" section
[2] See instructions on how to bottle butter in "storing perishable foods" section

- 3 cans pork & beans or other canned beans
- 1 c. BBQ sauce
- 1 c. brown sugar
- ½ c. ketchup
- 1 apple-- sliced[1]
- ¼ c. golden raisins

Mix all together, bake at 350 for 30-40 minutes.

BBQ Sauce

Food Storage Items:

- ½ cup Karo syrup
- ½ cup ketchup
- ½ cup finely chopped onion
- ¼ cup cider vinegar
- ¼ cup Worcestershire sauce
- ¼ cup mustard

Mix together ingredients in a small saucepan. Bring to a gentle boil for 15 minutes or until sauce thickens. Enjoy.[2]

BBQ Sauce- quick version

Food Storage Items:

- 1 c. Ketchup
- 1 c. Brown Sugar
- 1 T. Lemon juice

---

[1] Can use dried apples
[2] This is the recipe for basic BBQ sauce, you can add seasonings as you like such as honey, brown sugar smoke flavor etc.

This is a quick and easy sauce for stir-fry or Chinese cooking. Adjust the ingredients to your liking. [1]

BBQ Shredded Chicken Sandwiches

Food Storage Items:

- Bottled chicken[2]
- Bottle of BBQ sauce
- Homemade bread[3]

Warm up the chicken and BBQ sauce. Spoon onto sandwich bread or rolls.

Best Brownies

Food Storage Items:

- 2 c. sugar
- 1 c. flour
- 1 c. butter[4]--melted
- 2/3 c. cocoa powder
- ½ t. baking powder
- ½ t. salt
- 4 eggs[5] (or gelatin egg substitute)
- Pam spray

---

[1] Additions such as honey, smoke flavor etc. can also be added.

[2] See instructions on how to bottle chicken in the "canning meats" section

[3] See homemade bread recipe

[4] See instructions on how to bottle butter in "storing perishable foods" section

[5] See recipe and instructions for egg substitute in "storing perishable foods" section

Mix all well. Pour into greased pan. Bake at 350 for 23 minutes or until set.

Biscuits

Food Storage Items:

- Bisquick
- Milk[1]
- Pam spray

Make according to directions on the box. If you are storing this separate from the box make sure to type up the directions and any other needed information.

Biscuits from Scratch

Food Storage Items:

- 2 c. flour
- 1 T baking powder
- 1 t. salt
- 1 T sugar
- ¼ c. shortening
- 1/3 c. milk[2]

Mix dry together, cut in shortening and mix well. Add milk. Knead until not sticky. Cut into circles. Bake at 425 for 13-15 mins.

---

[1] Use made-up powdered milk
[2] Use made-up powdered milk

Bread

Food Storage Items:

- 2 T yeast
- 1 T sugar
- 1 cup water (luke warm)

Dissolve in bowl-- let sit

In another bowl, mix:
- ½ c. sugar
- ½ c. oil
- 4 t. salt

Add yeast mixture, then add:
- 4 cups hot water
- 4 cups flour

Beat in about 7 more cups of flour

Let rise 1 ½ hours, shape in loaves. Bake at 350 for about 35 mins or until golden brown. Can be used for scones or rolls as well.

Breadstick Seasoning

Food Storage Items:

(I usually double this recipe and keep it in an old Parmesan cheese bottle):

- 1/2 c. Parmesan cheese
- 2 t. salt
- 2 T. garlic powder
- 2 t. oregano
- 2 t. basil

- 2 t. marjoram
- 2 t. parsley

Mix together. Does not have to be refrigerated, but you can for a longer shelf life.

Butter Cream Frosting

Food Storage Items:

- 1 cube (1/2 c.) butter[1]
- 2 c. powdered sugar
- 1 t. vanilla
- ½ t. salt
- ¼ c. evaporated milk

Soften but do not melt butter. Mix all together until desired consistency. For thicker frosting add more powdered sugar. For chocolate frosting add cocoa powder, or for another flavor add 1-2 t. flavored extract (orange, mint, raspberry etc.). You can always add food coloring to make it the desired color as well.

Butterscotch Brownies

Food Storage Items:

- 1 ½ cubes butter[2]
- 2 c. brown sugar

Melt, cook till bubbly. Cool for 5 minutes. Add:

---

[1] See instructions on how to bottle butter in "storing perishable foods" section
[2] See instructions on how to bottle butter in "storing perishable foods" section

- 3 eggs [1]
- ½ t. vanilla
- 1 ½ c. flour
- 1 c. coconut
- 1 ½ t. baking powder
- 1 c. pecans or walnuts[2]
- ¼ t. salt

Pour into a 9x13" greased and floured pan. Bake at 350 for 22-25 minutes. Dust with powdered sugar.

Butterscotch Bubble Loaf

Food Storage Items:

- 1 small box instant butterscotch pudding
- ½ c. pecans-- chopped[3]
- ½ c. butter-- melted[4]
- ½ c. brown sugar
- Bread dough rolled into roll sizes[5]

Heat butter and brown sugar until melted into a syrup. Spray bunt pan with pam, layer; rolls, pudding (dry) & nuts. Pour syrup over top. Cover and let raise to double. Bake at 350 for 30-35 minutes (cover with foil for the first 15 minutes).

---

[1] See recipe and instructions for egg substitute in "storing perishable foods" section

[2] See instructions on how to bottle nuts in "storing perishable foods" section

[3] See instructions on how to store nuts in "vacuum packing" section

[4] See instructions on how to bottle butter in "storing perishable foods" section

[5] See recipe for bread

Cake

Food Storage Items:

- Cake mix[1]
- Oil or applesauce
- Gelatin as egg substitute[2]
- Pam spray

Follow directions on box using the gelatin egg substitute recipe in place of the eggs. Applesauce can be used instead of oil.

Cake- super easy soda cake

- Cake mix[3]
- 1 can of soda pop

Mix cake mix and soda pop together then pour into the pan and bake until golden. You can use different types of cake mix and soda such as: chocolate & cola, strawberry & strawberry-kiwi soda, white & root beer and so on.

---

[1] See instructions on how to vacuum-pack mixes for longer shelf life in "vacuum packing" section
[2] See recipe and instructions for egg substitute in "storing perishable foods" section
[3] See instructions on how to vacuum-pack mixes for longer shelf life in "vacuum packing" section

Cake Mix Cookies

Food Storage Items:

- Box of cake mix (any kind)[1]
- Gelatin egg substitute for 2 eggs[2]
- ¼ c. oil or applesauce
- Pam spray
- Tub of frosting (optional)

Mix well, and roll into balls and place on a greased cookie sheet. Bake at 350 for 8 minutes. You can frost 2 cookies together if you want and make a sandwich cookie.

Caramel

Food Storage Items:

- 1 c. sugar
- 1 c. brown sugar
- 1 c. light Karo syrup
- 1 c. butter[3]
- 1 can sweetened condensed milk[4]

Combine all and cook over med-high heat, cook to a easy softball stage for caramel popcorn, and a medium softball stage for caramel candy.

---

[1] See instructions on how to vacuum-pack mixes for longer shelf life in "vacuum packing" section

[2] See recipe and instructions for egg substitute in "storing perishable foods" section

[3] See instructions on how to bottle butter in "storing perishable foods" section

[4] See recipe for homemade sweetened condensed milk if no canned product is available

Cobbler

You can make it with any fruit you like-- and it works with canned pie filling, or just a can of that fruit!
Food Storage Items:

- 1 can of fruit or pie filling (any kind)
- 1 box of cake mix [1] any flavor
- 1 can of Sprite or 7-Up soda
- Cinnamon or nutmeg (optional)

Spread the fruit in the bottom of the pan. Sprinkle the cake mix on top. Pour the soda on the cake mix, then lightly mix the soda and cake mix with a fork being careful not to go all the way down to the fruit. Sprinkle with cinnamon or nutmeg if desired. Bake at 350 for 35 minutes or until golden brown and set.

Chicken Pot Pie

Food Storage Items:

- Bottled chicken[2]
- 1 can cream of chicken soup
- 1 can corn, green beans, peas, carrots, and any other veggies you like
- 1 c. Bisquick mix
- milk[3]

Mix together chicken, veggies, and soup. Pour into a casserole pan. In a separate bowl mix Bisquick with enough milk to make

---

[1] See instructions on how to vacuum pack mixes for longer shelf life
[2] See instructions on how to bottle chicken in the "canning meats" section
[3] Use made up powdered milk from your food storage

it thin like a pancake batter. Pour the Bisquick batter on top of the chicken & veggie mixture. Bake at 325 for 1 hour.

Chicken & Rice Casserole

Food Storage Items:

- Rice
- Bottled chicken[1]
- Can of corn
- Can of green beans
- 2 cans of cream of chicken soup
- Ritz crackers to top
- Water

Cook rice in water. Add all other ingredients but Ritz. Sprinkle Ritz on top. Bake at 350 for 30 minutes.

Chicken Salad (for sandwiches)

Food Storage Items:

- Bottled chicken[2]
- ½ c. mayonnaise
- ¼ c. mustard
- Poppy seed dressing

---

[1] See instructions on how to bottle chicken in the "canning meats" section
[2] See instructions on how to bottle chicken in the "canning meats" section

Mix chicken, mayo, and mustard together. Spread on croissant cut in half or bread. Pour poppy seed dressing on top, top with bread or croissant.

Chili

Food Storage Items:

- Bottled ground beef[1]
- 2-3 cans of beans (any kind you like)
- 3 cans stewed tomatoes
- 2 cans tomato sauce
- 1 can tomato paste
- 1 T. Italian seasoning
- 1 can mushrooms (optional)

Mix all in a pan and heat up.

Chocolate Chip Cookies

Food Storage Items:

Cream together;
- ½ cup butter[2]
- ½ cup brown sugar
- ¼ cup sugar

Add the following to the sugar mixture:
- 1 egg[3]

---

[1] See instructions on how to bottle ground beef in the "canning meats" section

[2] See instructions on how to bottle butter in "storing perishable foods" section

[3] See recipe and instructions for egg substitute in "storing perishable foods" section

- ½ tsp vanilla

Add to mixture and beat together:

- 1 ½ cup flour
- ½ tsp baking soda
- ½ tsp salt
- ½ cup chocolate chips[1]

Mix well. Bake at 375 for 10-13 minutes or until golden brown.

Chocolate Chunk Cookies

Food Storage Items:

- box chocolate fudge cake mix[2]
- 1 ¼ c. semi-sweet chocolate chips[3]
- 2 large boxes chocolate fudge pudding mix

Add:

- ½ c. chopped walnuts[4]
- 1 ½ c. mayo

Shape into balls, put on ungreased cookie sheet. Bake at 350 for 10-12 minutes. Makes 48 cookies.

---

[1] See instructions for storing chocolate chips in "storing perishable foods" section

[2] See instructions on how to store mixes in "storing perishable foods" section

[3] See instructions on how to store chocolate chips in "storing perishable foods" section

[4] See instructions on how to store nuts in "storing perishable foods" section

Chocolate Truffles

Food Storage Items

- 3 c. semi-sweet choc. chips[1]
- 1 can sweetened condensed milk[2]

Melt together, and then add:
- 1 T vanilla

Mix well. Refrigerate 2-3 hours. Roll into balls, then roll in powdered sugar or other topping (crushed nuts, coconut, cocoa powder, etc.)
Refrigerate.

Cornbread

Food Storage Items:

- 1 pkg. yellow cake mix[3]
- 1 c. flour
- 1 t. baking powder
- 1/3 c. shortening
- 1 c. milk[4]
- 1 c. cornmeal
- 3 T. sugar
- 1 t. salt
- 1 egg[5]

---

[1] See instructions for storing chocolate chips in "storing perishable foods" section
[2] See recipe for sweetened condensed milk if not available
[3] See how to store in "vacuum packing" section
[4] Use made-up powdered milk
[5] See recipe and instructions for egg substitute in "storing perishable

Prepare cake mix to direction. Save ½ for cupcakes or double rest of the recipe. Combine dry ingredients. Cut in shortening. Beat egg and milk together, add to dry, add cake batter. Blend well. Bake at 375 in cupcake pan or loaf pans.

Corny Fritters

Food Storage Items:
- ½ c. corn meal
- 1/3 c. shortening
- 1 ¾ c. milk[1]
- 1/3 c. sugar
- 2 t. salt

Cook above until thick in sauce pan-- cool. Add:
- ¾ c. creamed corn
- 2 eggs[2]
- 1 T yeast dissolved in ¼ c. warm water

Mix. For Fritters-- roll and cut like scones, then fry. Shake in a brown paper bag with powdered sugar. For rolls or bread let rise 10 minutes, then bake until golden.

Cranberry Orange Oatmeal Cookies

Food Storage Items:

- 1 c. butter-- softened[3]

---

foods" section

[1] Use made-up powdered milk

[2] See recipe and instructions for egg substitute in "storing perishable foods" section

[3] See instructions on how to bottle butter in "storing perishable foods" section

- 1 c. brown sugar
- 1/2 c. sugar

Cream all together then add:

- 2 eggs[1]
- 1 1/2 t. vanilla
- 1 t. orange extract
- 1 1/2 c. flour
- 1 t. baking soda
- 3 c. oatmeal
- 1 c. dried cranberries

Bake at 350 for 10-12 mins or until golden.
(the original recipe also called for 1 T of orange zest, but I didn't have an orange)

Dirt Dessert

Food Storage Items:

1 large box instant chocolate pudding
2 c. milk[2]
2 cups chopped Oreo cookies[3]
Gummy worms[4]

Prepare pudding according to box. Pour into either individual cups or one bowl. Sprinkle Oreos (dirt) on top. Stick gummy worms in to look like they are coming out of the dirt.

Enchiladas with White Sauce

---

[1] See recipe and instructions for egg substitute in "storing perishable foods" section
[2] Use made-up powdered milk
[3] Recommended to store in air-tight container such as Tupperware for best freshness.
[4] See instructions on how to store candy in "vacuum packing" section

Food Storage Items:

Sauce, combine all and heat in a saucepan:
- 1 can cream of chicken soup
- 1 can cream of mushroom soup
- 1 can diced chilies
- 16 oz sour cream[1]

- Bottled ground beef or chicken[2]
- Tortillas[3]
- Cheese (optional)[4]

Heat up tortillas till soft. Heat up ground beef. Spoon some sauce into a large pan to coat the bottom. Roll meat, 2 T sauce, and sprinkle of cheese (optional) in each tortilla. Pour remaining sauce on top of all enchiladas, sprinkle cheese on top (optional). Bake at 350 until golden.

English Toffee

Food Storage Items:

- 1 # butter (4 cubes)[5]
- ½ c. water
- 2 c. sugar
- Pam spray
- 2 c. milk chocolate chips[6]

---

[1] Powdered sour cream can be purchased and used
[2] See instructions on how to bottle ground beef in the "canning meats" section
[3] See recipe for tortillas
[4] Frozen shredded cheese or Velveeta can be used
[5] See instructions on how to bottle butter in "storing perishable foods" section
[6] See instructions for storing chocolate chips in "storing perishable foods" section

Mix butter, water, and sugar. Cook over med heat until golden brown.

Pour into a greased cookie sheet. Immediately top with or milk chocolate chips and spread once the chocolate is melted. Sprinkle with 1 c. nuts (optional).

French Dressing

Food Storage Items:
- 1 can tomato soup
- ¾ cup vinegar
- 1 tsp salt
- ½ tsp paprika
- 1 T Worcestershire
- ½ tsp pepper
- 1 T minced onion
- 1 T dry mustard
- 1 ½ cup salad oil
- 1 clove garlic (optional)

Mix in quart jar. Shake to use. Mix in blender for creamy French dressing.

Frosting

Food Storage Items:

- 2 cups powdered sugar
- ½ cup white shortening
- 4 TBSP hot milk

Mix with hand blender about 10 minutes.

Granola Bars

Food Storage Items:

4 ½ c. rolled oats
1 c. flour
1 t. baking soda
1 t. vanilla
2/3 c. butter-- softened[1]
½ c. honey
1/3 c. brown sugar
1 ½ c. mini chocolate chips-- or other add in of your choice (nuts, marshmallows, etc.)[2]

Mix together, press into greased 9x13": pan. Bake at 325 for 18-22 minutes. Cut into bars.

Heinz Ketchup (copycat recipe)

Food Storage Items:

- 1 (6 ounce) can tomato paste with garlic
- 1/2 c. light corn syrup
- 1/4 c. white vinegar
- 1/4 c. white balsamic vinegar
- 1/4 c. water
- 1 T. sugar
- 1 t. salt
- 1/4 t. onion powder

Combine all and cook until boiling. Simmer for 30 minutes stirring often.

---

[1] See instructions on how to bottle butter in "storing perishable foods" section
[2] See instructions for storing chocolate chips in "storing perishable foods" section

Hot Cocoa Mix

Food Storage Items:

- 32 c. powdered milk
- 2 c. non-dairy creamer
- 2 c. powdered sugar
- ½ c. cocoa
- 11 oz quick mix (Nestle quick)

Mix all together, store in air-tight container. Use 4 T per cup.

Hot Fudge Sauce

Food Storage Items
- 1 c. butter[1]
- 1/3 c. unsweetened cocoa powder
- 3 c. white sugar
- 12 oz. can evaporated milk
- 1 t. vanilla

Combine all BUT vanilla, bring to a boil for 7 minutes. Remove from heat, add vanilla. Put in blender & blend for 2-4 minutes.

Lemon Bars

Food Storage Items:
Crust:
- 1 c. soft butter[2]

---

[1] See instructions on how to bottle butter in "storing perishable foods" section

- Dash of salt
- ½ c. powdered sugar
- 2 c. flour

Press into 9x13" pan and bake at 350 for 15 minutes.

Filling:
- 4 eggs [1]
- 2 c. sugar
- ¼ c. flour
- 6 T. lemon juice

Bake for 25 minutes until set. Sprinkle top with powdered sugar.

Mac & Cheese

Food Storage Items:
- Boxed mac & cheese
- Water
- Milk[2]
- Butter[3]

Make according to instructions on box. As a variation you can add bottled ground beef to the mac & cheese.

Macaroni Tuna Salad

Food Storage Items:
- 3 c. (12 oz)macaroni noodles
- 1 can peas-- strained

---

[2] See instructions on how to bottle butter in "storing perishable foods" section

[1] See recipe and instructions for egg substitute in "storing perishable foods" section

[2] Use made-up powdered milk

[3] See instructions on how to bottle butter in "storing perishable foods" section

* 1 can carrots-- strained
* 1 can tuna-- strained
* 6 T mayo
* 2 t. All Seasoning
* 1 t. salt or onion salt
* 1 t. garlic salt
* water

Cook noodles. Mix all together.

Magic Cookie Bars

Food Storage Items:

* 10 graham crackers-- crushed
* ½ c. butter--melted[1]
* 1 can sweetened condensed milk
* 2 c. chocolate chips[2]
* 2 c. coconut
* 1 c. nuts (optional)[3]

Melt butter in the bottom of a pan. Sprinkle graham crackers on top of butter. Layer the rest of the ingredients. Bake at 350 for 25-30 minutes.

Mayonnaise

---

[1] See instructions on how to bottle butter in "storing perishable foods" section

[2] See instructions on storing chocolate chips in the "vacuum packing" section

[3] See instructions on storing nuts in the "vacuum packing" section

Food Storage Items:

- 1 egg[1]
- 1/2 teaspoon minced garlic
- 1 tablespoon lemon juice
- 1 teaspoon prepared yellow mustard
- 3/4 cup vegetable or olive oil[2]
- salt and pepper to taste

Combine the egg (or egg substitute), garlic, lemon juice and mustard in the container of a blender or food processor. Blend until smooth, and then blend on low speed while pouring oil into the blender in a fine stream as the mixture emulsifies and thickens.

Mayonnaise Cake

Food Storage Items:

- 1 c. sugar
- 1 ¾ c. flour
- 1 c. raisins
- 1 t. cinnamon
- 1 c. chopped walnuts
- 1 t. baking powder
- 1 t. baking soda
- ½ t. allspice
- 1 c. boiling water
- ½ t. nutmeg
- 1 t. vanilla

---

[1] See recipe and instructions for egg substitute in "storing perishable foods" section

[2] Olive oil is a healthy alternative, seasonings can also be added for extra flavor

- 2 T. cocoa
- 1 c. mayo
- ½ t. salt

Sift flour, spices, salt, cocoa and baking powder together 3 times. To this add the sugar, nuts and raisins. Dissolve soda in boiling water, make sure it fizzes. Add hot mixture to dry mixture. Then stir in vanilla and mayo (not salad dressing). Bake at 350 for about 40 minutes, test and ice with your favorite icing.

Mustard

Food Storage Items:

- 1/2 cup dry mustard powder
- 1/2 cup white vinegar
- 1 teaspoon salt
- 1/2 teaspoon pepper
- 2 tablespoons white sugar
- 3 egg yolks, beaten[1]

In a heavy saucepan combine mustard, vinegar, salt, pepper and sugar. Simmer over low heat for 3 hours. Beat egg yolks into mixture and stir until thickened. Pour into hot, sterilized jars and seal. Cool at room temperature and store in the refrigerator.

Navajo Tacos

Food Storage Items:

- Homemade bread dough[2]

---

[1] See recipe and instructions for egg substitute in "storing perishable foods" section

[2] See recipe for food-storage ingredients

- Bottled ground beef[1]
- Taco seasoning mix
- Water
- Sour cream[2]
- Canola or vegetable oil

Heat oil up. Stretch dough out into flat rounds about 4" in diameter. Cook dough in oil until golden. Heat up ground beef; add taco seasoning and ½ c. water. Top each golden scone with taco meat. Add water to sour-cream powder then scoop sour cream on top of taco meat.

No-Heat Truffles

Food Storage Items:

- ¾ c. powdered sugar
- 1 tub chocolate frosting
- 1 t vanilla or other flavored extract

Mix well. Spoon onto plate, sprinkle with cocoa powder. Refrigerate 15 minutes.

Noodle Salad (Chicken or Tuna)

Food Storage Items:

- Bottled chicken[3] or can of tuna

---

[1] See instructions on how to bottle ground beef in the "canning meats" section

[2] Can be found in a freeze-dried powder form for shelf-stable food storage

[3] See instructions on how to bottle chicken in the "canning meats"

- Noodles-- any size/shape
- Water
- Can of peas
- 1 c. Mayo or other dressing (I use a Vidalia onion dressing sometimes with the chicken)

Cook noodles in water. Mix remaining together with noodles.

Oatmeal Cookies

Food Storage Items:

- 1 c. butter[1] --melted
- 1 c. sugar
- 1 c. brown sugar
- 2 eggs[2]
- 1 t. vanilla
- 2 c. flour
- 1 t. baking powder
- 1 t. salt
- 2 ½-3 c. oatmeal
- 2 c. chocolate chips[3] or dried cranberries & 1 t. orange extract (all are optional)
- Pam spray

---

section
[1] See instructions for bottling butter in "storing perishable foods" section
[2] See recipe and instructions for egg substitute in "storing perishable foods" section
[3] See instructions on storing chocolate chips in the "vacuum packing" section

Mix all together, spoon onto greased cookie sheet. Bake at 350 for 8 minutes.

Pancakes

Food Storage Items:

- Bisquick or pancake mix
- Gelatin egg substitute[1]
- Milk[2]

Prepare according to directions.

Peanut Butter Bars

Food Storage Items:

- ¾ c. margarine[3]
- ¾ t. baking soda
- ¾ c. brown sugar
- ½ t. vanilla
- ¾ c. sugar
- 1 ½ c. flour
- 2 eggs[4]
- 1 ½ c. oats
- ¾ c. peanut butter
- ½ t. salt

---

[1] See recipe and instructions for egg substitute in "storing perishable foods" section
[2] Use made-up powdered milk
[3] You can use butter-flavored Crisco instead of margarine which has a long shelf life
[4] See recipe and instructions for egg substitute in "storing perishable foods" section

Mix well. Spread on a large cookie sheet. Bake at 350 for 15 minutes.
Whip 1 c. peanut butter and spread on hot bars. Cool, then spread with chocolate icing:

- ½ c. margarine-- melted[1]
- ½ c. cocoa powder
- 1/3 c. evaporated milk
- 1 2/3 c. powdered sugar (approx)
- 1 t. vanilla

Beat until smooth.

Peanut Butter & Jelly Sandwich

Food Storage Items:

- Peanut Butter
- Jelly or Jam[2]
- Sliced bread[3]

Spread each onto a slice of bread

Pizza Factory Breadsticks (or as close as I've seen!)

Food Storage Items:

- 1 1/2 c. warm water
- 1 T. yeast

---

[1] You can use butter-flavored Crisco instead of margarine which has a long shelf life
[2] See instructions on making jam in the "bottling fruits" section
[3] See recipe for bread

- 2 T sugar

Mix and let set to dissolve for 5 minutes, then add:

- 3 1/2 c. flour
- 1 t. salt

Mix till smooth and not sticky. Let rise for 10 minutes. Roll out flat, cut strips, then roll each strip in to a long rope, fold rope in half and twist. Place on a cookie sheet. Spread melted butter on top of each bread stick, then sprinkle seasoning[1] on top. Let rise for 15 minutes.

Bake at 400 for 7-10 minutes. Butter and season again if needed.

Posse Stew

Food Storage List:

- Bottled ground beef[2]
- 1 can Mexican or Italian stewed tomatoes (I chop in blender)
- 1 can ranch style beans
- 1 or ½ small can mild chopped green chilies
- 1 can corn
- 2 T Worcestershire
- 4 T bacon bits (optional)

Simmer.

---

[1] See breadstick seasoning recipe
[2] See instructions on how to bottle ground beef in the "canning meats" section

Pumpkin Chocolate Chip Cookies

Food Storage Items:

- 1 box spice cake mix
- 1 small can pumpkin
- 1 cup mini chocolate chips
- Pam spray

Mix cake mix and pumpkin until smooth (will be dry at first), add chocolate chips. Spoon onto a greased cookie sheet and bake at 350 for 8 minutes – do not overbake! (sometimes takes some practice to adjust to your oven) it's better to take these out a little early and let them set-up-- then they will be nice and soft.

*VARIATIONS: you can use chocolate cake mix for chocolate pumpkin cookies

Ranch Dressing

Food Storage Items:
- 2 c. mayo
- ½ t. garlic powder
- 2 ½ T. dry parsley
- ¾ t fresh ground pepper
- 1 t. salt
- 2 c. buttermilk[1]
- 1 t. onion powder
- ½ t. MSG (optional)

Mix & set in fridge uncovered overnight.

Rice-a-Roni Chicken Salad

---

[1] Can be bought in powder form

Food Storage Items:

- Bottled chicken[1]
- Box of rice-a-roni
- 1 c. mayonnaise
- 1 T. Worchester
- ½ c. celery & green onions[2]
- Water

Cook rice-a-roni according to directions. Mix all together. Serve warm or cold.

Rice Crispy Treats

Food Storage Items:

- 6-9 c. rice crispy cereal
- Marshmallows[3]
- 1 cube (1/2 c.) butter[4]

Melt butter in a large pan on stove. Add marshmallows, once marshmallows are melted turn off heat and add rice crispy cereal. The more cereal the more dry and crunchy they will be, less cereal will make them soft and chewy.

Rice Pudding

---

[1] See instructions on how to bottle chicken in the "canning meats" section

[2] If available. You can get these in freeze-dried form.

[3] Recommend storing in air-tight container such as Tupperware

[4] See instructions for bottling butter in "storing perishable foods" section

Food Storage Items:

- 4 ½ c. milk[1]
- ½ c. uncooked rice
- 1/3 c. sugar
- ½ t. salt
- ½ c. raisins
- vanilla/cinnamon

Combine first four ingredients and pour into greased baking dish. Cover and bake at 325 for 45 mins, stir every 15 minutes. Add raisins, vanilla, and cinnamon. Cover and bake 15 minutes more.

Sausage Gravy (serve over biscuits)

Food Storage Items:

- Bottled sausage[2]
- 2 T butter[3]
- 2 T flour
- 2 c. milk[4]
- Seasonings[5]

Heat up sausage, add butter. Once butter is melted add flour, mix well, and then add milk slowly. Cook until thickens, add

---

[1] Use made-up powdered milk
[2] See instructions on how to bottle sausage in the "canning meats" section
[3] See instructions for bottling butter in "storing perishable foods" section
[4] Use made-up powdered milk
[5] According to your taste

seasonings as needed. Recommended seasonings: chicken bouillon, salad seasoning, seasoned salt, and/or garlic & herb.

Shepherd's Pie

Food Storage Items:

- Bottled ground beef[1]
- 2 cans tomato soup
- 1 can green beans
- 1 package of mashed potato mix
- Water

Mix ground beef, soup, and green beans together. Pour into the bottom of a casserole dish. Mix mashed potato mix with hot water (a little more water than called for so it's thinner than normal), pour potatoes over the meat mixture. Bake at 350 for 20 minutes.

Sloppy Joe Biscuits

Food Storage Items:

- Biscuits[2]
- Bottled ground beef[3]

---

[1] See instructions on how to bottle ground beef in the "canning meats" section
[2] See recipe for biscuits
[3] See instructions on how to bottle ground beef in the "canning meats"

- 1 bottle BBQ sauce
- Cheese-- optional[1]

Warm up ground beef & BBQ sauce. Place biscuit dough in the bottom of a cupcake pan, spoon meat mixture on top of dough, then place biscuit dough on top of the meat. Top with cheese (optional). Bake at 350 for 18 minutes or until biscuit is golden.

Spaghetti

Food Storage Items:

- Spaghetti noodles
- Bottled ground beef[2]
- Bottled spaghetti sauce[3]
- Water

Boil noodles, heat up ground beef and add sauce.

Stroganoff

Food Storage Items:

- Bottled chunks of beef[4]
- Noodles

---

section

[1] If you have shredded cheese in the freezer, or want to use a Velveeta kind

[2] See instructions on how to bottle ground beef in the "canning meats" section

[3] Store- bought or homemade-- see recipe section for canning homemade sauce

[4] See instructions on how to bottle beef chunks in the "canning meats" section

- 2 T. butter[1]
- 2 T. flour
- 2 c. milk[2]
- Seasonings-- beef bouillon, Worchester, dried onions, etc.
- Water
- Sour cream (optional)[3]

Cook noodles. In separate pan heat up the meat, add butter and once it's melted add flour. Mix together well, and then slowly add milk. Add any seasonings you like. Add noodles and serve with a scoop of sour cream on top (optional).

Stuffing Casserole

Food Storage Items:

- Box of stuffing mix
- Can cream of chicken soup
- Can of corn
- Can of Green beans
- Cereal flakes (such as Total or Special K) or Ritz crackers

Mix first 4 together; sprinkle crushed cereal or Ritz on top. Bake at 350 for 30 minutes.

Sweetened Condensed Milk

Food Storage Items:

---

[1] See instructions for bottling butter in "storing perishable foods" section
[2] Use made-up powdered milk
[3] Sour cream can be bought in powdered form

- 1 c. powdered milk
- 1/3 c. boiling water
- 2/3 c. sugar
- 3 T butter[1]

Combine all in a blender and mix on low speed for 1 minute. Increase speed and mix until sugar is dissolved and is smooth. This recipe equals one store bought can of sweetened condensed milk.[2]

Sweet & Sour Pork

Food Storage Items:

- Bottled pork chops
- Cook enough rice for your family
- 1/2 of a large can of pineapple
- 1/2 c. ketchup
- 1/4 c. brown sugar
- 2 T. honey
- 2 t. cornstarch

Mix well until it starts to thicken up, add 1/2 of the can of pineapple, then serve over rice.

Sweet Potato Casserole

Food Storage Items:
- 2 cans sweet potatoes
- 1 c. milk[3]

------

[1] See instructions for bottling butter in "storing perishable foods" section
[2] Recipe from "Not your mother's food storage" –Kathy Bray and Jan Barker

- ½ t. cinnamon
- ¼ c. sugar
- 2 eggs[1]
- ¾ stick butter--melted[2]
- ½ t. nutmeg

Mix well and bake in greased pan at 400 for 30 mins

Topping:
- 1 c. brown sugar
- 1 ½ c. corn flakes-crushed
- 1 c. pecans
- 1 ½ sticks butter-melted[3]

Mix well, then top over casserole and cook for another 15 minutes.

Tartar Sauce

Food Storage Items:

- 1 c. mayo
- 1 T. sweet pickle relish
- 2 T. lemon Juice

---

[3] Use made-up powdered milk

[1] See recipe and instructions for egg substitute in "storing perishable foods" section

[2] See instructions for bottling butter in "storing perishable foods" section

[3] See instructions for bottling butter in "storing perishable foods" section

Mix and serve with fish-- best if refrigerated 1 hour before serving.

Thousand Island Dressing

Food Storage Items:

- 8 c. mayo
- 1 c. tomato puree
- 1 12-oz sweet pickle relish (drained)
- 6 hard-boiled eggs (put in when you use it)
- Seasoned salt
- Touch of cayenne pepper or 2 shakes Tabasco sauce
- 2 T. onion powder
- Chopped green olives (optional)

Mix well.

Thumbprint Cookies

Food Storage Items:

- 1 c. butter[1]
- 2/3 c. sugar

Cream together, then add:
- ½ t. almond or vanilla extract
- 2 c. flour

Mix and roll into balls. Press thumb into the middle-top to make a little dip. Then pour a spoonful of jam into each hole.
- ½ c. raspberry jam (or any other jam)

Bake at 275 for 14-18 minutes

---

[1] See instructions for bottling butter in "storing perishable foods" section

Tortillas[1]

- 4 cups all-purpose flour
- 1 teaspoon salt
- 2 teaspoons baking powder
- 2 tablespoons shortening[2]
- 1 1/2 cups water

Whisk the flour, salt, and baking powder together in a mixing bowl. Mix in the shortening with your fingers until the flour resembles cornmeal. Add the water and mix until the dough comes together; place on a lightly floured surface and knead a few minutes until smooth and elastic. Divide the dough into 24 equal pieces and roll each piece into a ball.

Preheat a large skillet over medium-high heat. Use a well-floured rolling pin to roll a dough ball into a thin, round tortilla. Place into the hot skillet, and cook until bubbly and golden; flip and continue cooking until golden on the other side. Place the cooked tortilla in a tortilla warmer; continue rolling and cooking the remaining dough.

Trifle

Food Storage Items:

- White or angel food cake mix
- Oil or applesauce

---

[1] This recipe is from www.allrecipes.com Lard was changed to shortening
[2] Crisco stores well and can be used for any recipes calling for shortening

- Gelatin egg substitute[1]
- Strawberry Jell-O
- Water
- Instant vanilla pudding
- Milk[2]
- Whipping cream[3]

Make Jell-O according to package directions. Let set up. Make cake according to directions using gelatin egg substitute. Let cool. Cut up cake into chunks and place on top of Jell-O. Make pudding according to directions. Pour pudding over cake & Jell-O. Make whipping cream according to directions. Pour over Jell-O.

Tuna Fish Gravy on Toast

Food Storage Items:

- 3 T Butter[4]
- 4 T Flour

Melt in sauce pan
Slowly add:
- 2 c milk [5]

Add milk slowly, stirring constantly. If milk is added too quickly it will result in lumpy gravy.

---

[1] See recipe and instructions for egg substitute in "storing perishable foods" section
[2] Use made-up powdered milk
[3] Can also be purchased in powder form-- mix up according to directions
[4] See instructions for bottling butter in "storing perishable foods" section
[5] Use made-up powdered milk

***At this point you have basic gravy or thickening sauce; you can add seasoning/meats etc. too for other recipes.**
Add:
- 3-6oz cans tuna fish
- Salt and pepper to taste

Serve over toast or rice.

Tuna Sandwich

Food Storage Items:

- Can of tuna
- 1/3 c. mayo
- 3 t. lemon juice
- 1 T sweet relish (optional)
- Celery[1] (optional)
- Sliced bread[2]

Mix all together, spread on sliced bread.

Whole Wheat Bread

Food Storage Items:

- 7 c. white flour
- 4 T. yeast
- 2 T. salt
- 1 c. brown sugar

Mix well (you can add 1 c. bran or ½-1 c. wheat germ)
Add:

------

[1] You can purchase freeze-dried celery
[2] See recipe for bread

- 3-4 c. wheat flour

Knead 3-5 minutes until moderately stiff dough
Rise until double-- 30-40 minutes; punch down and let rest 10 minutes on floured counter. Divide into 4 loaves and place in greased pans. Let rise for 30-40 minutes. Bake for 40 minutes at 350.

Non-Food Recipes

All Purpose Cleaner

In a squirt bottle combine:

Water

2 T Dawn dish soap

Mix together. This is a great cleaner used for stains, grease, etc. on every surface I've tried! (if you're unsure test on a small area first)

Disinfectant cleaner

Water

Vinegar (about a 1:10 ratio- 10 cups water 1 cup vinegar)

Lemon essential oil –a few drops

Mix together and use on floors, counters, or bathrooms.

Disinfectant cleaner 2

Place orange or lemon peels in a jar with 3 cups water and ½ c. vinegar. Let sit for a few days and then strain out the peels and use in a spray bottle.

Homemade Fabreeze

1/8 Cup Fabric Softener
2 Tablespoons Baking Soda
Hot Tap Water - Fill the Bottle to the Top (32oz bottle)

To get rid of Fruit Flies

Place a inch or so of apple cider vinegar and a couple drops of dish soap into a small cup.

Homemade Laundry Soap- Powder

1 bar soap (you can also use fels-naptha or Zote)- shaved

1 c. Arm & Hammer washing soda

½ c. 20 mule team borax

Mix together well. Use 1-2 T per load

You may also add essential oils for scent (optional)

Laundry soap- liquid

1 bar of soap (any kind you want)
1 cup of Borax
1 cup of washing soda
a big pot (that holds more than 2 gallons)
a grater
a funnel

a long spoon
2 empty gallon jugs/containers

Grate your soap and add it to 1 gallon of water. Cook until soap dissolves, then add in borax and washing soda. Bring to a boil (will get thicker) Remove from heat and add 1 gallon of cold water. Mix well, then pour into your container(s). Use ½ cup of this per load.

Lamb or baby animal formula

2 c milk
1 egg
1 T karo syrup
1 T corn oil
5-6 drops baby vitamins (optional)
Heat and blend together well.

Laundry Stains

Put some dawn dish soap directly on the stain before washing.

Skunk Smell

2 things to try that are effective at getting out skunk smell are:

1) 2 parts of hydrogen peroxide & 1 part baking soda
2) Tomato juice

Spider repellant

Bounce fabric sheets can be used to deter spiders, mosquitoes, and other pests. Just place a few sheets in areas where you see these pests the most.

Resources

www.atozformomslikeme.blogspot.com

www.gossner.com

http://www.livingoffgrid.org/pressure-canning-chart-foods-processing-times-psi-and-elevation/

http://www.gopresto.com/recipes/canning/fruits.php

http://www.recipetips.com/kitchen-tips/t--1396/canning-temperatures-and-processing-times.asp

www.ebay.com

Wendy Dewitt, Everything under the sun
(http://www.youtube.com/watch?v=HhGaTlwYs-s)

Wendy Dewitt, Everything under the sun blog
(http://everythingunderthesunblog.blogspot.com/)

"Not your mother's food storage" –Kathy Bray and Jan Barker

"Home Storage: Build on the Basics", Ensign, June 1989, 39

Letter to priesthood leaders, 24 June 1988

"That Noble Gift—Love at Home," *Church News,* May 12, 2001, 7

"To Men of the Priesthood," *Liahona and Ensign*, Nov. 2002, 58

"If ye are prepared ye shall not fear," Ensign, Oct. 2005

www.allrecipes.com --homemade flour tortillas, mustard, mayo

Some of my recipes were from family members: my grandmas, my mom, Monica & Jill.

http://www.canning-recipes.com/

www.ehow.com – how to make & use a solar oven

Freeze-drying process: Shelf Reliance Staff, Sept 22nd 2009 See more at www.shelfreliance.com

For more information:

www.facebook.com/groups/foodstorage101

www.what8ate.com

www.what8ate.thrivelife.com

www.facebook.com/what8ate

www.atozformomslikeme.blogspot.com

www.facebook.com/atozformomslikeme